Prai
The Trifecta of Trust

"There's nothing more vital to leadership and collaboration than trust, and Joseph Folkman has spent his career becoming a trustworthy source of knowledge and data on it. His book is filled with practical insights for earning, keeping, and repairing trust."

—**Adam Grant,** #1 *New York Times* bestselling author of
Think Again, host of the podcast *WorkLife*

"Building trust is perhaps the greatest leadership capability of all. Joe's wonderful book explains what trust is all about and serves as a guidebook for understanding and developing trust in your leaders, your organization, and yourself."

—**Josh Bersin,** global industry analyst

"Joe Folkman has done it again with *The Trifecta of Trust*! Take the guesswork out of building trust in your teams and organizations and learn the bad behaviors that are holding you back from your full potential. Well researched and full of practical advice, every leader needs to read this book!"

—**Dr. Marshall Goldsmith,** Thinkers50 #1 executive coach, *New York Times* bestselling author of *Triggers, Mojo,* and *What Got You Here Won't Get You There*

"Brilliant work! Based on research insights (not just personal opinions), Joe has established the primary elements of trust and shown their impact on numerous outcomes. This is a foundational work for individuals, leaders, and organizations seeking results through trust."

—**Dave Ulrich,** Rensis Likert Professor, Ross School of Business, University of Michigan, partner, The RBL Group

"You might be brilliant, strategic, ambitious, and hardworking . . . but if you're not trusted, you've got nothing. This book gives you the data-tested insights that will help you build a foundation for success."

—**Michael Bungay Stanier,** bestselling author of
The Coaching Habit and *How to Begin*

"While everyone acknowledges the importance of trust, it has remained vague, even a bit mysterious. Based on multiple research studies involving thousands of global leaders, the mystery is unshrouded. Most important, the reader receives numerous suggestions on ways by which they can become more trusted in every realm of their work and life. Unhesitatingly recommended reading!"

—**Jack Zenger,** CEO, Zenger Folkman

"A great leadership books delivers three things: it cuts through the clutter to show you what's most important now, transforms your perspective to clearly see what the heck is going on, and provides pragmatic coaching advice to help you improve. *The Trifecta of Trust* does all this and one more: it's backed up with amazing research and insightful analysis. From teamwork to DEI to agility, this book will help any leader looking for fresh thinking and proven solutions to the most vexing problems and promising opportunities we face today."

—**Kevin D. Wilde,** Executive Leadership Fellow, Carlson School of Management,
University of Minnesota, former chief learning officer, General Mills Inc.

"At first, I was surprised to see that Joe was writing about trust. I've known Joe a very long time. Joe is a data guy. But the power of this book is that Joe shifts trust from a qualitative conversation to one that is grounded in real data. This book is worth the read, and I'd recommend it to anyone who wants to learn what to do to improve their trustworthiness with others as well as those responsible for developing leaders where learning how to increase trust is important. Basically everyone."

—**Norm Smallwood,** cofounder, The RBL Group

"Few things are as critical today to leadership, and life, as building and restoring trust. Joe Folkman's exceptional book, *The Trifecta of Trust*, provides the research-based tools to actually do it. Trust transforms and so will this book!"

—**Kevin Cashman,** global coleader of CEO & Enterprise Leader Development, Korn Ferry, bestselling author of *Leadership from the Inside Out* and *The Pause Principle*

"You won't be able to read this book without some serious self-reflection: what am I doing to create (or diminish) trust in the most important relationships I have? The good news is that the secrets to improving trust are given to us—with *The Trifecta of Trust*."

—**Kathleen Stinnett,** MCC and certified coaching supervisor, founder of FutureLaunch, coauthor of *The Extraordinary Coach: How the Best Leaders Help Others Grow*

"Trust must be earned, trust can be lost, but trust can also be rebuilt. Read this book—and learn from a great expert."

—**Anne Esling,** chief people & culture officer at Clarins, Paris, France

"Any experienced leader knows the importance of trust: if your team doesn't trust you, it is impossible to be effective. Using his vast database from decades of research, Dr. Joe Folkman points out how a struggling leader can rebuild the trust of the team, using clear language, great examples, and data-driven options for improvement. This book should be in the hands of anyone hoping to increase their leadership skills."

—**Paul McKinnon,** cofounder, The McKinnon Company, former CHRO, Dell Computers and Citigroup, former faculty, Harvard Business School

"The book really unveils very simple but practical ways to build and restore trust (if it is lost). I strongly recommend this book because it will surely bring any interested reader a lot of value and enlightenment."

—**Le Pham,** chairwoman, Le & Associates JSC., Vietnam

The
TRIFECTA
of
TRUST

The **PROVEN FORMULA** *for*
BUILDING *and* **RESTORING TRUST**

JOSEPH R. FOLKMAN

RIVER GROVE
BOOKS

Published by River Grove Books
Austin, TX
www.rivergrovebooks.com

Distributed by River Grove Books

Design and composition by Greenleaf Book Group and Mimi Bark
Cover design by Greenleaf Book Group and Mimi Bark
Cover images used under license from ©Shutterstock.com/Gwoeii

Publisher's Cataloging-in-Publication data is available.

Print ISBN: 978-1-63299-528-5

eBook ISBN: 978-1-63299-529-2

First Edition

Contents

Preface

More than 40 years ago, I became fascinated with the idea that behaviors could be measured. As I experimented with measuring behaviors, I discovered a way I could evaluate whether a measurement was accurate. If the behavior I measured predicted a valued outcome, if the behavior was improved, and if the outcome improved, it was a behavior that mattered. Most of the behaviors I measured were related to leadership, and the outcomes they produced touched everything from productivity, profitability, and discretionary effort to turnover, employee engagement, and customer satisfaction. Over time, I refined the behaviors that I measured, and I collected data from millions of assessors and hundreds of thousands of leaders from across the globe.

My life's mission has been to provide accurate assessments for leaders to understand their level of effectiveness and their impact on outcomes, and to provide them with insights on what they can do, specifically, to improve. Most people want to improve, but their approach often relies on conventional wisdom, such as fixing or hiding weaknesses, working harder, applying yourself, and focusing. Conventional wisdom is often not helpful because people simply do not know what to do to be more effective. After creating hundreds of assessments that measured leaders' effectiveness, I looked at all the data I had collected to discern the most effective assessment items. These differentiating items were the best at separating poor leaders from great leaders. The data started to reveal secrets about which behaviors were most important and how leaders could improve.

My partner, Jack Zenger, and I wrote a book called *The Extraordinary Leader*. The book focused on the difference in outcomes between being a good leader and being a great leader. Great leaders doubled profits, the engagement of employees, and the satisfaction of customers.

Over time, I grew interested in which individual small behavior would have the largest impact. This was my Manhattan Project. The atom is so small, but its impact can be so enormous. After years of analysis, I discovered that the atom of leadership is trust. Trust is a very small issue. Most people think they know if they are trusted (but they are often wrong). They know who they trust and who they do not trust, but this one small issue can positively or negatively affect everything else you do. If you give a speech and people trust you, they listen and accept. But if they do not trust you, they reject and revolt.

You can assess trust across the world by asking just one question: "Can most people be trusted?" The percentage of people in a country who answer in the affirmative can predict the wealth and prosperity or poverty and crime of that country. If trust is low, business slows down, people want more assurances, both parties are suspicious of the other party, and ultimately, prosperity is also low. Trust is the atom of leadership because it impacts everything.

After studying data from over a million assessments of hundreds of thousands of leaders, I discovered the three elements that either build or destroy trust. I wrote this book to help people understand how to control and harness the power of the atom of trust.

And after measuring the effectiveness of those hundreds of thousands of leaders, two further insights have become perfectly clear to me. First, leaders do not really know how effective or ineffective they are. Second, they do not understand the impact their behavior has on others. This book is intended to help you open your eyes to the potential damage your own behavior may cause. But more important, it is intended to help you fix it.

Introduction

"Learning to trust is one of life's most difficult tasks."

—ISAAC WATTS

In 1429, France was in the thick of the Hundred Years' War with the English. Paris had already been taken, and King Charles VII was exiled. Hope was lost, and it would take a miracle for the French to keep their land. That miracle manifested in the scrawny form of a teenage girl illegally dressed as a man who claimed angels were speaking to her, commanding her to save her people.

She had no training, she was the wrong gender, and she was too young. Yet, with no record of any questioning of her leadership, she led an army of hardened and exhausted soldiers into Orleans and took back the city from the English. Stories of her powerful influence are recorded, detailing her troops' celebrations over her arrival on the day of battle. With her at the helm, they were willing to go anywhere. The army, once in despair and discouraged, redoubled their efforts and would often end the day victorious. Historians account that military finances also improved under her leadership, and people genuinely believed in the cause they were fighting for. Within a year of the Orleans victory, she managed to return King Charles VII to the throne and was an important presence at the coronation. No small feat for a peasant girl from the country.

The war continued, and she continued to fight until she was captured by the English and burned at the stake for heresy, dressing like a man, and witchcraft. After her death, King Charles VII declared her a martyr for the cause, and she has remained a symbol of hope for the French people until this day. In 1920, she was officially canonized by the Catholic Church and is revered as a patron saint of France. You can even see a shrine dedicated to her in Notre-Dame cathedral.

Joan of Arc would not have accomplished anything if her troops did not trust her. She would have been just a person yelling at the top of her lungs at a bunch of people. But her troops *did* trust her. They trusted her with their lives, with their king, and with their country.

The exiled king trusted her and even appointed her to a military position. He believed her stories of divine revelation after having theologians test her, deeming her consistent in her purity, chastity, and piety. Her victory in Orleans proved to the country that she was a good leader, allowing her to continue leading. She lost some battles, but her troops never lost hope with her at their lead until her eventual capture.

On the other side of the globe, Abraham Lincoln led the United States through its darkest hour—a fissure that looked as if it would never heal. Tall and soft-spoken, he failed many times politically and financially before winning the presidency, but those loyal to the Union trusted him.

He effected huge change. He led the country through a war that killed more Americans than any other conflict before or after; enacted the Emancipation Proclamation, effectively freeing thousands of enslaved people; and then united the South and the North into a coherent whole, despite major trauma and cultural frustration. We revere him to this day for his leadership and unwavering dedication to the Union. Politicians on both sides of the aisle seek to emulate him and be positively compared to him, and he is considered one of the greatest presidents of all time.

Both Joan of Arc and Abraham Lincoln led masses of people through incomparable fear, loss, and change while managing to keep their reputations unsullied. Of course, both of these heroes made mistakes, but they were easily forgiven in the moment and even now, as history looks fondly on them. We forgive them easily because we already love them, we trust their intentions, and we are determined to honor their legacies.

Most of us are not in the middle of uniting America or saving our entire country from a fifteenth-century foe. Our battlefield is the office, and our soldiers are our employees. We have all heard this metaphor a trillion times, but it remains relevant. These are uncertain times: ongoing economic crises, new and insurmountable health crises, technological advances that upend our systems and processes, new laws and expectations. The very fabric of our world continues to change at a faster and faster rate. Within our office walls, each of us is experiencing immense amounts of stress and anxiety in addition to our daily obligations. We need leaders who can lead their people through these complications. In fact, we actually need to *be* those leaders.

Becoming an effective leader requires trust. It doesn't matter how smart you are or how revolutionary your ideas are, but it does matter if your people do not trust you. You need generals and infantry to wage any battle, and these people must invest significant amounts of trust to risk their lives (or careers) following your lead. Earning, building, and maintaining that trust is a crucial part of any leader's arsenal.

We all have felt trusted by others, and to our chagrin, we have also felt moments when we were not trusted. We can relate to experiences when someone we did not know well was trying to sell us something, and the thought crossed our mind, *Do I trust this person enough to give them my money?* We also may have bought something and, in looking back, realized that it was a huge mistake.

Accumulating these experiences, most people form theories about trust. These theories answer the basic questions, *Who can and who cannot be trusted? How can you get others to trust you?* and *What can you do to rebuild the trust that is lost?* These theories are what I call *observational* theories.

Jerry Seinfeld is the master of observational humor. He looks at the everyday experiences we all have in our lives and then points out how strange or odd those experiences are when examined closely. His comedy is unique and relatable to everyone. For example, he says one thing that makes us all feel safe and connected today is a rectangular object in our pocket: a mobile phone. Our mobile phones were designed to stay connected with the people in our lives, but no one wants to talk anymore, because they prefer social media, games, texting, or scrolling mindlessly.

In the same way, observational theories are theories based on personal experiences. They feel relatable, but they might not actually be accurate. Some are excellent descriptions of what is actually happening, but others are entirely wrong. Many people *do* use cell phones to stay connected and to talk to their friends even more than they would have without them. Access to social media can actually build community. Although Jerry Seinfeld's observational humor feels true, it might not actually be a good representation of what is going on around us.

The vast majority of the books on trust are observational. When we read them, they make a lot of sense, and in fact, they are full of common sense, but there is no way to know if it is excellent wisdom or worthless nonsense. There is no statistical backing or documented anthropological pattern that we can point to in order to justify the findings; it is usually just a bunch of hearsay.

This book is based on the analysis of data. Rather than asking you to believe in my observational expertise, my goal is to show you the results that provide evidence of the impact of different behaviors on trust. I am going to give you actual patterns and numbers you can rely on.

There will be a lot of numbers, percentiles, and graphs in this book, but I invite you to remember that these numbers are people. They represent leaders working in the mining industry in Canada, in biotech and educational institutions across Europe, in the agriculture and manufacturing industries of Mexico, and in the banking and finance enterprises in the United States. The data collected represents thousands of organizations in various places around the world. Yes, it is a number, but that number represents the collective human experience and struggle of leaders to build and maintain trust.

While there could be hundreds of behaviors that impact trust, just three can account for the vast difference in the impact of individuals with high levels of trust and those who are not trusted at all. These are the core behaviors that create and reinforce trust from others:

- displaying expertise and the good judgment that comes with it,
- demonstrating consistency, and
- building relationships.

These three pillars support the foundation of trust, regardless of culture, industry, race, or gender.

It's hard to describe the remarkable impact that comes when a person is trusted or when the trust that was lost has been restored. The connection of trust binds people together not just for a job assignment but for a lifetime. Through these statistics and examples, I hope to illustrate the impact of trust and a clear path for you to follow. Improving trust with others will help you be more successful, loved, appreciated, and valued.

CHAPTER 1

The Impact of Trust

If we are going to understand a behavior as complex as trust, we need to dissect how it can affect an individual's career. Many of my colleagues joke about my love for my "golden database." Indeed, I have earned my 10,000 hours time and time again by poring over millions of 360-degree feedback reports from thousands of leaders. Inside these reports are clues about developing trust from the experiences of leaders and employees around the world.

Let's start by introducing some tools I use to evaluate performance and trust. The 360-degree feedback report was first introduced while I was in graduate school. Three of my professors created a list of items and asked managers, peers, direct reports, and others to evaluate the effectiveness of another manager. The key to making this work well is that the feedback from peers, direct reports, and others would all be kept confidential, requiring at least three respondents in order to show the ratings.

After my professors tested the process, they hired me to go and sell this evaluation tool to large companies. As I would sit down and explain the process to potential clients, they would often react by saying, "So you are going to ask direct reports to evaluate their manager? That's the opposite of the way we have managed people." Their observation was correct, but we had discovered that those direct reports were very effective and consistent in their evaluations of which managers were highly effective and which ones needed significant improvement. We also found that most of the managers had no clue whether they were the next in line to become the CEO or next to be laid off.

Over the years, this 360-degree feedback process, done the right way, has moved from an oddity to a fairly common practice in many organizations. In measuring the impact of 360-degree feedback, my studies have shown that the majority of leaders who participate in the process make a significant improvement in their leadership effectiveness over an 18-to-24-month period.

Once the 360-degree feedback is gathered, the results are compiled into a feedback report. To create an effective 360-degree assessment, I researched more than 2,000 items generated from more than 1.5 million raters to identify the behaviors that were the most effective at differentiating between poor leaders and great leaders. The items cluster into groups of three to four behaviors that measure a competency.

Such 360-degree assessments will evaluate both managers' and individual contributors' effectiveness on anywhere from 6 to 19 competencies. In the feedback report, a participant can see their results and compare them to norms. I like to show others how they compare to the global norm of others at the 75th and 90th percentile (i.e., the best leaders). In our Extraordinary Leader 360-degree assessment,[1] we measure 19 competencies, which cluster into five broad dimensions:

---

1   Trust is one behavior in the builds relationships competency. For additional information on this competency
    model and the latest research, I strongly recommend the book *The New Extraordinary Leader* by Jack Zenger and
    Joseph Folkman.

- Character (honesty and integrity)
- Focus on results (drive for results, taking initiative)
- Interpersonal skills (builds relationships, communicates, inspires)
- Personal capability (technical expertise, problem solving)
- Leading change (strategic perspective, champions change)

While the exact percentiles vary according to the competency, the following is a general guide.

- A score in the 90th percentile or above means an individual has an *outstanding strength* in a competency.
- A score in the 75th percentile indicates they have a *strength*.
- A score in the 50th percentile indicates they are *competent*.
- A score in the 40th percentile indicates they need *some improvement*.
- A score in the 10th percentile indicates they need *significant improvement* and have a fatal flaw.

As you look through the data presented throughout this book, you can use these markers as a guide.

THE IMPACT OF TRUST FOR THE LEADER

After evaluating one of Zenger Folkman's clients (I'll call him Bill), I realized that Bill was a leader most organizations would be eager to hire. He possessed outstanding strengths in such enviable leadership skills as championing change, establishing stretch goals, and driving for results. I imagined he might be a talented leader, a general leading his troops up the hill to battle. He immediately explained that I was incorrect. In fact, none of his troops were even willing to consider walking up the hill behind him. He had one significant weakness: His team definitely did not trust him.

At the top of his feedback report was the comment that no leader wants to receive and that would be hard to forget: "Bill always delivers results, regardless of the cost or the dead bodies left behind."

Bill's team clearly knew that, to him, results were more important than the people doing the work. He was willing to go to battle, but his soldiers were terrified that they would be sacrificed along the way.

What follows is a look at Bill's 360-degree assessment results that he received on 16 leadership competencies (Figure 1.1). I invite you to adopt a Sherlock Holmes mindset as you read through the report.

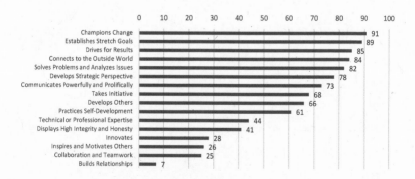

Figure 1.1: Bill's 360-degree assessment results.

Why Did Bill Receive This Negative Feedback?

Bill hit the 91st percentile on a very important competency, championing change. He was close to the 90th on two additional competencies, establishing stretch goals and driving for results. But with a score for building relationships in the 7th percentile, it was clear that he had a significant flaw. Fatal flaws don't kill leaders, but they can kill their careers.

Bill had the potential to be one of the best leaders I have ever met, but his lack of trust left him with direct reports who had employee satisfaction and engagement scores in the 20th percentile. The majority of his direct reports were looking outside the organization for other jobs, and none of his team members were willing to go the extra mile; his team did what they needed to do to keep their job but nothing extra. The fact that Bill got anything done was remarkable, because with scores that low he was running alone.

After looking through his results for an hour, I checked in with Bill and asked him for his thoughts. Bill looked at me and said, "Well, this is only what my direct reports think, but I know other people trust me."

I asked if he had a family.

He said, "Yes, I do, and I know they trust me."

I asked Bill to take a break and call his wife, tell her about his results, and ask her if there were times when she felt the same way. Bill came back after the call and said that his wife agreed that sometimes she did not trust him. He made the mistake of asking for examples, and the call lasted much longer than 10 minutes.

Bill then looked straight at me and said, "I have two questions. Can this be fixed? If so, how?"

These questions are not uncommon. Trust is an issue that goes beyond organizations and is a critically important thread in the fabric of health for countries, communities, and families.

THE IMPACT OF TRUST FOR EMPLOYEES

Sometimes, a lack of trust isn't isolated to an individual. It may be a part of the corporate culture of an organization. Paul Zak, an American neuroeconomist, studied the differences between high-trust organizations and low-trust organizations. In an economic paper, he looked at the differences between high-trust and low-trust cultures. He found that cultures having high levels of trust had less friction. Friction is created when it is difficult to get others to agree or cooperate, and it eases when getting things done is quick and simple. There is a great deal of friction in low-trust cultures, but high trust reduces the friction, which makes it easier for economic activity to flourish. He also found that there was a lower probability of people defaulting on their commitments in high-trust cultures. Trust was an excellent predictor of a country's economic prosperity or poverty. Poorer countries had lower levels of trust, and more prosperous countries had significantly higher levels of trust, less friction, and fewer defaults.[2]

He also discovered that one way to assess trust was to draw blood and measure the level of oxytocin. Higher levels of oxytocin in a person's brain are associated with increased trust and empathy. A person who is stressed has significantly lower levels of oxytocin. While drawing blood and measuring the levels of oxytocin provided useful data, doing broader studies with larger populations using this approach would create significant problems. Who wants to have their blood

---

2   Paul J. Zak and S. Knack, "Trust and Growth," *The Economic Journal* 111, no. 470 (March 2001): 295–321.

drawn to measure the levels of oxytocin directly after a stressful meeting or a pleasant performance review?

Based on his research, Zak was able to develop a survey assessment that measured the level of trust in organizations. He found that employees in high-trust organizations reported the following:

- 40 percent less burnout
- 66 percent more closeness with colleagues
- 50 percent higher productivity
- 13 percent fewer sick days
- 106 percent more energy at work
- 70 percent more alignment with the company's purpose
- 17 percent higher compensation than their peers in low-trust companies
- 29 percent more satisfaction with their lives[3]

Zak's research in this assessment focused on a high-trust culture. Think about working in an organization where there is low trust, resulting in a high level of burnout, conflict between employees, low productivity, people using all their sick days as vacation, no enthusiasm, and work feeling like a difficult chore, and add to that poor pay. People in this kind of a situation see top management as the enemy, and they view escape as their only option.

---

3 Paul J. Zak, *Trust Factor: The Science of Creating High-Performance Companies* (New York: Amacom, 2017).

DO YOU REALLY KNOW IF YOU ARE TRUSTED OR DISTRUSTED?

While we all preach the importance of trust in organizations, determining whether you are trusted is not always straightforward. A leader may be completely unaware that they are distrusted. Bill knew he was the best at driving for results (and yes, not everybody liked him because he wasn't a relationships guy), but he didn't realize that people didn't trust him.

This is something that you need to open your mind to consider: People may not trust you as well as you think they do. How do I know this? By looking at the self-assessments of leaders and comparing them with the scores from other raters. Raters other than the leaders themselves are, on average, 3.2 times better at predicting the right level of trust. This is so common that 27 percent of leaders overrated their levels of trust.[4]

While you may believe that the lack of awareness of trust issues has no consequences, certain leadership behaviors were dramatically impacted by this denial. This means that when colleagues did not trust a leader, they also perceived the leader to be less effective in various skills, but seven specific skills were hit the hardest. Figure 1.2 shows the wide gap in effectiveness scores between the leaders who didn't realize how highly they were trusted (underraters) and those who naively thought they had no problems (overraters).

The graph shows ratings from all raters (managers, peers, direct reports, and others) with the self-ratings excluded. People were divided into two groups: those who overrated themselves and those who underrated themselves. Notice the substantial differences in the scores between those who overrate and those who underrate their trust.

---

4   The study included global data from 83,836 self-assessments and 1,084,028 assessments in Zenger Folkman's database.

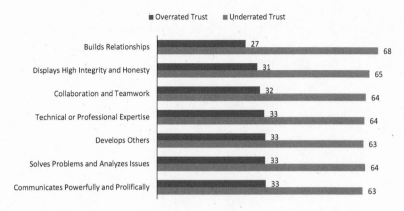

Figure 1.2: Top seven competencies most impacted by overrating trust.

These trust overraters were evaluated as having worse relationships, being less honest, collaborating poorly, and exhibiting less technical skill than they themselves believed. They also were rated as less able to develop others, solve problems, and communicate powerfully than they actually believed.

The shocking thing about this data is these behaviors are not just centered on relationships or interpersonal skills. It is not just about people not liking you. If you aren't trusted, when you offer a solution to a problem, people don't consider it seriously; they second-guess you. When you turn over your work on a project that you spent hours perfecting, they dismiss the quality. When you speak up about new ideas, policies, or processes, they could tune you out, and there is a 1-in-4 chance that you may not know it. Bill didn't know it. The far-reaching effects of a lack of trust can destroy a career and significantly damage your organization. Do I have your attention?

CHAPTER 2

Trust Makes
Everything Better

S alt changes the flavor of many foods—often in unexpected ways.
When I was young, I was once served fresh cantaloupe for dessert.
I was surprised to hear my father say, "Please pass the salt."

When I gave him a disgusted look, he suggested that I sprinkle salt on
my melon. To my complete surprise, the melon was made even sweeter.

This is not complex. Salt draws water to itself. If you bite in the vicin-
ity of the salt, the added flow of water brings more flavor, making the
cantaloupe taste sweeter. The salt does not add a new taste of its own. It
changes the chemical structure of the melon to bring out the flavor that
otherwise would be locked in the cantaloupe's cells.

Trust is a lot like salt. It doesn't necessarily add new flavor on its
own, but it enhances everything it touches. The data we've discussed
so far has shown that the effects of distrust on an individual's career,
a team's effectiveness, or an organization's culture can be widespread.

However, the data also demonstrated that while a lack of trust can inflict much damage, the presence of trust can provide far more benefits. Just as the addition of salt can enhance any food, trust has the ability to significantly elevate other leadership behaviors.

POWERFUL COMBINATIONS

As I studied the impact of trust in different industries, I noticed something unusual happening when I combined the results with other leadership behaviors.

In a study I published in *The Extraordinary Leader*, I found that certain combinations of leadership behaviors can significantly boost different outcomes, such as leadership effectiveness and employee engagement. For example, take the combination of drives for results and relationship building. If a leader had an outstanding strength at relationship building but struggled with driving for results, the chances of being perceived as a great leader were only 9 percent. On the flip side, if that leader was outstanding at driving for results and bad at relationship building, the chances went down to 8 percent. However, when a leader had a strength in both skills—driving for results and relationship building—the probability of being a great leader shot up to 82 percent. That leap is the profound effect of a powerful combination of behaviors.

I just did not know how profound this was in terms of trust. Trust is different.

I first discovered that when a high level of trust was combined with great communication skills, employee engagement moved up 24 points, to the 76th percentile (see Figure 2.1).

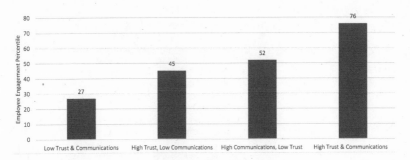

Figure 2.1: The powerful combination of trust and communication skills, and effect on engagement.

This powerful combination made sense. Consider what happens when a person has a leader who communicates well, keeps the team informed, and delivers messages others understand, but when trust is lower than desired. Even though the direct reports understand the leader's messages, they may question the leader's motives, and ultimately, their commitment is reduced.

TRUST AND OTHER LEADERSHIP COMPETENCIES

I wondered if trust would have the same impact on other leadership competencies. As I ran the numbers, I was surprised to see a powerful combination happening again, and again, and again. I ran the data, looking at 16 leadership competencies. When a high level of trust was added to each of the competencies, the average increase in effectiveness ratings on each competency went up 23 percentile points. For all of the competencies listed in Figure 2.2, the addition of high trust moved a competency's effectiveness above the 70th percentile, and for 15 of the competencies, into the top quartile.

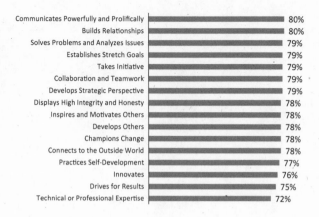

Figure 2.2: Percentage of leaders at the 90th percentile
when competencies combine with trust.

Trust reaches in and changes the way other people respond to a leader. It identifies and validates the leader's motivation for all other behaviors. It appears to impact all other behaviors because it tells an employee whether their boss is acting out of self-interest. It assures them that they are not being hoodwinked or taken advantage of.

Through analyzing each of these behaviors, I was beginning to see an unknown, underappreciated, and invisible influence trust had on boosting employee engagement. Where else did this invisible force elevate its leaders?

TRUST AND OVERALL LEADERSHIP EFFECTIVENESS

In another study of global leaders, I looked at the overall leadership effectiveness rating, which is based on the 360-degree assessment ratings of 49 behaviors found to differentiate great leaders from poor leaders. I found that if a leader has a trust rating in the bottom 10th percentile, their average overall leadership effectiveness rating is at the

14th percentile. Leaders with the highest level of trust (those in the top 10 percent) have an overall leadership effectiveness rating at the 86th percentile. You can easily conclude from Figure 2.3 that a leader's overall effectiveness is driven by the extent they are trusted.

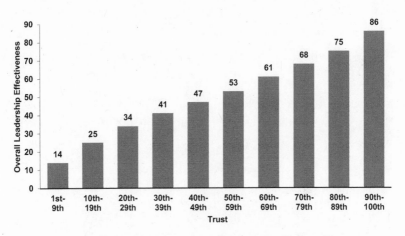

Figure 2.3: Impact of trust on overall leadership effectiveness. Scores are based on group of 76,116 global leaders.

TRUST AND DISCRETIONARY EFFORT

Trust doesn't just affect the perceptions of a leader's overall greatness; it influences employees to do more. Discretionary effort is basically an individual's commitment to put extra time and effort into their job. Many employees are only willing to do the minimum amount of work necessary to keep their jobs. If employees are willing to put in the additional effort, that means increased productivity for the organization.

In this same group of leaders, I measured the level of trust that direct reports had for their managers, along with their willingness to go the extra mile. For the leaders with the lowest level of trust, only 17 percent of their employees were willing to go the extra mile. For the leaders with the highest level of trust, 58 percent of their employees were willing to give extra effort.

Most people at some point in their lives have been part of a team where people were more willing to give extra effort. The esprit de corps in those teams increases not only productivity but also the enjoyment of the job. An employee in a high-discretionary-effort team once told me, "We thought that what we were doing would change the world, and it did!"

Leaders who are trusted can change the world for those around them. And I don't mean just the ones in the history books, like Joan of Arc or Abraham Lincoln. Leaders like Bill, who want to do their best and are desperate to find a way to help their teams trust them, can also vastly improve their team's world.

ENHANCING LEADERSHIP FLAVOR

That was a lot of numbers. I warned you at the start, but these numbers should give you hope. My message, based on this analysis, is this: Whatever skill or capability might be your strength, if you can understand trust and increase it, then that skill will be enhanced and the outcome improved.

Leaders who are trusted have significantly higher levels of leadership effectiveness and inspire greater discretionary effort from their direct reports. Organizations with trust have less burnout and more energy. Trust is the glue that holds teams together, and its lack is the toxicity that tears them apart. Encouraging trust from your team is worth your time and effort.

CHAPTER 3

The Trifecta of Trust

One sweltering day in the summer of 1949, a lightning bolt set the grassy highlands in the Mann Gulch river valley of Montana on fire. Led by nine-year veteran Wag Dodge, a group of smokejumpers were dispatched to battle the growing fire. The conditions were bad, and with no radio or map of the terrain, the men were all alone. As the evening sun started to set, the conditions worsened, with the wind shifting and causing an inferno that was heading straight toward the men. The flames were now 200 feet high, 300 feet deep, and moving at 30 miles per hour.

Dodge frantically commanded the men to fall back and get rid of their heavy packs, but the fire was moving too fast for them to outrun it. Dodge had fought enough fires to know this fact, and that is why he stopped running and tried to get the other 15 men to do the same. His cries for them to stand still were ignored as they continued running in various frantic paths. They were desperate to escape and unsure of Dodge's strange instructions. In a moment of pure inspiration, Dodge had come up with a plan that Jonah Lehrer described in his book *How We Decide.*

> He quickly lit a match and ignited the ground in front of him. He watched as those flames raced away from him, up the canyon walls. Then Dodge stepped into the ashes of this smaller fire, so that he was surrounded by a thin buffer of burned land. He lay down on the still smoldering embers. He wet his handkerchief with some water from his canteen and clutched the cloth to his mouth. He closed his eyes tight and tried to inhale the thin ether of oxygen remaining near the ground. Then he waited for the fire to pass around him. After several terrifying minutes, Dodge emerged from the ashes virtually unscathed.[5]

The Mann Gulch fire ended up claiming the lives of 12 of the 15 smokejumpers who went to fight it that day. Dodge and two other men (who successfully found a crevice in a rocky hillside) were the only survivors. This is a story that numerous thought leaders have analyzed because of its many layers. While I can only speculate on the details described in later reports, I think heavily on the responsibility that Dodge had to his men and why they didn't put their trust in him. If they did, they would have lived.

The research I'm sharing is not solely teaching you how to help others trust you more; trust also must flow in the opposite direction. You need to understand how to put more trust in others, how to let go of control and acknowledge the trust issues that get in the way of your performance and your team. Trust goes both ways. You need to earn it, and you need to give it. While a lack of trust may only rarely

---

5   Jonah Lehrer, *How We Decide* (Boston: Houghton Mifflin Harcourt, 2009).

result in the loss of precious life, its influence on day-to-day functions is prevalent.

How you establish trust with your coworkers, friends, partner, spouse, children, or family members rests on three essential pillars.

THREE PILLARS OF TRUST

The first pillar of the trifecta of trust is *expertise*. This is the extent to which you are well informed and knowledgeable. It includes your understanding of the technical aspects of the work, as well as your depth of experience. Expertise is demonstrated foremost by a leader who uses good judgment when making decisions. With expertise, others trust your ideas and opinions and seek them out. This pillar is built on your knowledge, and your expertise makes an important contribution to achieving results. Expertise allows you to anticipate and respond quickly to problems.

Once you have achieved a level of expertise, you must demonstrate *consistency* in your knowledge and judgment. Consistency is the second pillar that builds trust. Consistency involves the extent to which you walk the talk and do what you say you will do. That means that you set a good example and are a good role model for others on your team and mentees. You honor your commitments and keep promises, and you follow through on both. It typically means that you are willing to go above and beyond what needs to be done.

The final pillar of trust is *fostering positive relationships*. This is often shown through staying in touch with the issues and concerns of others. You will also balance results with concern for others, rather than focus only on a goal, as Bill did. Your relationships will generate cooperation and will help in resolving conflicts. Within positive relationships, you can be counted on to consistently give honest feedback in a helpful way. In order to maintain these strong bonds, you will need to build an inclusive climate for those who think differently.

THE IMPACT OF THE THREE PILLARS

Often in my research on leadership, I tell people that they don't need to be perfect to be an excellent leader. To have a high level of trust, all three pillars need to be above average.

The tragic story of Wag Dodge's team in the Mann Gulch fire illustrates the importance of all three of the trust pillars. Most of the young men with him that day were just teenagers working a summer job. While they acknowledged Dodge's expertise and experience, they did not know him well enough to see consistent behavior. And when it came down to trusting him with their lives, the relationships weren't there. While Dodge's technique of burning a safe spot is now standard practice for firefighters, in that desperate moment, to those men, it seemed absolutely crazy. William Hellman, who was the second-in-command, reportedly responded to Dodge's risky plan by saying, "To hell with that, I'm getting out of here." Hellman led some of the men up a ridge, and he was the only one to get across it, but he died the next day from third-degree burns.

It's impossible to know how anyone will react in a life-or-death situation. I can only assume that if these men had trusted Dodge more and if he had been able to build the relationships necessary to gain that trust, then they would have listened to him instead of giving in to their uninformed instincts or following the second-in-command.

Everyone will have moments in their lives or careers when they will be asked to give up some control and put their trust in someone. In addition, you may someday be the one pleading for those around to follow you on a path that may be risky or never tried before. This level of trust requires all three of these pillars.

When I looked at the trust levels of the leaders around the world, it became clear that if a leader scored in or above the 60th percentile on all three factors, their overall trust score was in the 80th percentile. This means that if a leader was barely above average on all three factors, their trust score would soar. This is not a brilliant level of performance; it's barely above average. Without doubt, a leader will be more skilled at one of these pillars than others. This also means that trust would be damaged if a leader scored just below average on any of these pillars.

CAN TRUST BE IMPROVED?

We all want and need to believe in second chances. Once trust is lost, can it be restored? Perhaps we believe too much in Jane Austen's words penned for her prideful Mr. Darcy: "I find it hard to forgive the follies and vices of others, or their offenses against me. My good opinion, once lost, is lost forever."

Fortunately for humanity, the world is not completely full of Mr. Darcys. I gathered data on trust from a group of leaders who participated in a 360-degree assessment and a post-assessment given 18 to 24 months later. In this group of talented leaders, a large number of them received alarming scores on trust from their colleagues. Sadly, they possessed the dreaded fatal flaw in trust, with an overall trust score averaging for the group at the 6th percentile.

On the three pillars of trust, this fatal flaw group of 233 leaders scored in the

- 14th percentile in building relationships,
- 20th percentile in good judgment and expertise, and
- 20th percentile in consistency.

There was some substantial work that needed to be done with these leaders and those who worked with them. By focusing on these three areas over the next 18 to 24 months, this group moved their trust score from the 6th to the 38th percentile.

Their scores on the three individual pillars moved to the

- 45th percentile in building relationships,
- 46th percentile in good judgment and expertise, and
- 44th percentile in consistency.

Imagine feeling a level of trust from your team that is less than 94 percent of the rest of the world. That's a devastating amount of mistrust. It probably felt like a hole so deep that a person might not ever be able to escape. To move from the 6th percentile to the 38th percentile represents an enormous shift in trust. That shift moved people from "I can never trust you" to "I may be able to trust you." These leaders have not arrived at the ultimate place they want to be yet, but they have started the journey. This demonstrates that there is a payoff for working on improving trust. It shows that building or repairing trust isn't going to magically jump you to the 90th percentile in just a few weeks with some positive experiences. Trust takes time, but the gains from this fatal flaw group show that improvement—and *significant* improvement—is possible.

I also measured another group of 1,731 leaders who focused on building trust that started in a very different place. They were at the 43rd percentile. This meant that, overall, they were pretty trusted by their colleagues. However, with some focused effort, this group was able to turn their average trust into a strength by scoring on the post-test in the 70th percentile.

TRUST MATTERS

Most of us are not in situations like Wag Dodge, where our team members' lives are literally in our hands. But their work life and feelings about their job are absolutely in your hands. For leaders who were rated in the bottom 10 percent for trust, 48 percent of their direct reports were thinking about quitting their jobs. Your team members' mental, emotional, and physical well-being on the job matter, and the extent to which a leader is trusted creates either a positive environment or a situation where team members want to leave. Whether you have a fatal flaw or are just doing OK, you owe it to the people in your life to establish a strong foundation of trust.

CHAPTER 4

Expertise

Ken managed the technology of a small firm. The organization was highly dependent on systems and computers, so his role was essential. He had a scruffy beard, was always dressed as though he was ready to hike, and had a calm and cool temperament. He was never wishy-washy on any issue but, rather, was precise on the right and wrong approaches to take.

No one really knew where his impressive knowledge came from. Ken had no formal training, but there was never a problem that he could not solve. When problems occurred, he wouldn't jump to conclusions; instead, he had a calm "Let's see if we can figure this out" approach.

When Ken approached the leaders in the firm to request a major investment in new equipment, the request came as a big surprise. The senior leaders pushed back on whether this was needed immediately.

Ken's reply came back in an email and said simply, "Yes. We need to do this now."

Permission for the purchase was given that day. The senior leaders trusted Ken because of his expertise.

Expertise is a major step in building trust. Figure 4.1 shows the impact of high versus average skills in technical expertise across different levels of management. This study is based on a global database of 63,568 leaders. What is surprising in the findings is that the top-quartile skills in technical expertise had slightly more impact for leaders at the top of the organization than for individual contributors. This means that, although expertise is crucial for any employee, it is especially essential for leaders to be seen as knowledgeable and able to make good decisions.

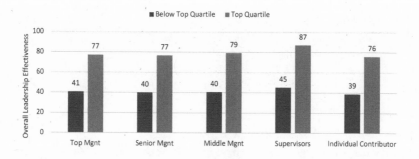

Figure 4.1: Overall effectiveness of leaders at different levels comparing top-quartile and below-top-quartile skills on technical expertise.

Many people struggle with this pillar, either because they have limited expertise and it feels impossible to build it or because they think they already are experts when they really are not. First, there are ways to increase expertise. Second, my research shows that an individual does not need to have all the expertise but, rather, the willingness to be a sponsor and showcase the expertise of others. They need to know enough and to be open to seek help from others to complement their own expertise. In other words, a person can be just as effective with limited knowledge, as long as they are humble enough to ask for advice or knowledge from others who are experts.

BEING AN INDIVIDUAL EXPERT

There are clear actions that help build skill in technical and professional expertise, as well as influence others' vision of you as the expert:

- Read additional journals and books.
- Subscribe and listen to relevant podcasts.
- Attend professional conferences.
- Enroll in university courses on technical subjects.
- Read the latest books published in the field.
- Participate in trade association meetings.
- Volunteer to speak at professional conferences or seminars.
- Become active in a professional organization.
- Explain to group members how new technology impacts the work of the company.
- Help integrate the different technologies that affect your group; determine how they fit together and how they contribute to the efforts of the organization.
- Define your role as facilitator and boundary manager for the

group and not as a lead expert among experts. Clarify this
role with the group.

- Ask a person who is an expert in this area to be a coach or
  mentor to you.

- Have lunch and learning sessions with recent university grad-
  uates where the latest trends and research are discussed.

- Visit and tour other companies who are on the cutting edge
  in your technical area.

Of course, it is impossible (or nearly impossible) to become an
expert in everything. Recently, I coached a leader working in a high-tech
organization who had very high scores on technical expertise. I complimented him on his results and commented that he must be a real expert.
I asked him, "So, what's your secret?" He said, "I just ask a lot of questions of my direct reports, get their opinions, and make sure they get all
the credit."

THE ARROGANT KNOW-IT-ALL
VERSUS THE HUMBLE EXPERT

I was giving a presentation with my colleague Jack Zenger several years
ago. After we finished, we opened the session to questions from the
audience. Jack and I both answered a variety of questions. Eventually,
a participant asked a question to which I did not have a good answer.
Immediately, I started to think of vague responses or some additional
questions—to answer a question with another question.

Jack jumped in and saved me. He said, "Well, this is a very bright group with years of experience. What do the rest of you think about this question?"

His answer prompted an excellent discussion, but Jack's response caused me to ask myself some tough questions. First of all, why did I feel compelled to have all the answers?

Often, when people are put in positions of authority, they believe that they need to have all the answers. Sometimes, these people think that they are the smartest person in the room, so they are highly motivated to constantly give their opinion and answer every question. Other times, they feel a strong sense of duty to know all the answers for what happens in their group or function. Do you often feel that you are responsible for having all the answers?

I did a study where we identified leaders who might not know themselves as well as they think. These were leaders who rated themselves in the top quartile on technical expertise, while those they worked with rated them in the bottom quartile. These leaders were also rated on the extent to which they acted arrogantly versus trying to listen and learn from others. I compared their results with those of leaders who were rated in the top quartile on expertise and also above average on humility. The overall leadership effectiveness rating is based on the average of 49 behaviors that differentiate poor leaders from great leaders.

In my analysis, I first looked at their overall leadership effectiveness rating from three groups: peers, direct reports, and their managers. As you can see in Figure 4.2, the arrogant know-it-alls were rated significantly more negatively by all three groups, but the peer differences were the largest. When peers at the same level interact with a person who assumes they have all the answers, their reaction is very negative.

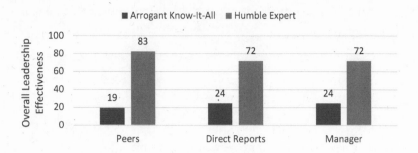

Figure 4.2: Overall effectiveness for peers, direct reports, and managers comparing arrogant to humble leaders.

Leaders who were arrogant know-it-alls were also rated significantly lower on how they were trusted (see Figure 4.3). Experts can build strong trust, but arrogant leaders whose expertise is fake destroy trust. In this graph, note the huge difference between the level of trust.

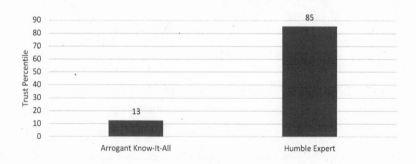

Figure 4.3: Trust, comparing arrogant with humble leaders.

Here's a dual case in point.

Jim was considered a high-potential leader and was doing well in his career. After a successful stint in R&D, the organization wanted to give him more breadth of experience, and he was appointed vice president of human resources. Jim had always thought of HR as a bunch of bureaucrats who got in the way of progress and results, but he realized this promotion was a test of his leadership capabilities.

The first week in the job, he gathered his functional heads together and had them each explain their duties and responsibilities. Every person in the group was an expert in their function, which made Jim feel confident that he could succeed. In his view, all they needed was some inspiration and they would all thrive. He did not feel a strong need to understand any of the functions that reported to him, because he knew the functional leader would keep things running well.

As Jim started to attend executive committee meetings with the CEO and his direct reports, Jim would give updates about HR. Occasionally, the CEO would ask for Jim's views on a new compensation process, changing the benefits, or a new approach to developing leadership talent. Jim had no shortage of ideas he would express in these sessions, and he would meet with each functional head after the meeting and tell them about the new direction the executive team had decided to take.

Often, the function group manager would be agitated and would explain that the new direction was a huge mistake, and Jim would just say, "The CEO wants to do this, so take your complaints to him personally." Eventually, a few brave managers did just that. They explained to the CEO why going in a different direction would be a significant problem.

It did not take long for Jim to get demoted and put back in R&D. Not only had he lost the trust of his direct reports, but he had also lost the trust of the CEO and his senior team.

Philippe had been in sales for most of his career. He loved the challenges that came from the sales function and had been very suc-cessful. Toward the end of Philippe's career, the CEO asked him to take over the human resources function. Reluctantly, he agreed but with a caveat: "I cannot be successful alone." Philippe took a month to learn all that he could from his functional heads. He would explain, "You are the expert; teach me what I need to know."

When attending executive meetings, Philippe had the motto "Never go to a meeting alone." He always brought a functional head to a meeting with him when he knew there would be a discussion relat-ing to one function. Philippe became a sponge, reading everything he could. Eventually, he saw a real need to develop the leadership talent in the organization. He discussed this with his functional head, and together, they created a plan. His functional head told him that no leadership development effort would be successful unless the senior leaders actively participated.

In a meeting with the executive team, Philippe agreed and got them all to agree they would be active participants in the process. After serving as the HR VP for two years, Philippe decided to retire. Every member of the executive team expressed their satisfaction with the job that he had done. Philippe had learned a great deal while in that position, but his reliance on his functional leaders had increased his expertise and the trust that every team member had in him.

COMPANION BEHAVIORS THAT HELP BUILD EXPERTISE

Now that you have mastered humility, consider other ways to increase your expertise.

Cross-training for related behaviors is one approach to widening your area of expertise. When athletes aspire to become more than just casual participants in a sport, they often turn to cross-training. Aspiring runners take up cycling, swimming, and weightlifting. Tennis players engage in long-distance running and weightlifting.

One way to explain this approach is that there is a strong, statistically significant correlation between people who are skilled cyclists and those who excel at running. Athletic trainers and coaches would explain this correlation by saying something about the cross-training activity strengthening the muscles used in the other activity or creating greater aerobic capacity or building general endurance, or they would give some other logical explanation. But the fundamental fact is that doing one thing has been shown to help people do others effectively.

When it comes to leadership development, a handful of specific behaviors are statistically significantly linked to each other. Leaders who got high scores on one behavior got high scores on the other behaviors; the ones that got low scores got low scores on those same behaviors. In some cases, the link between behaviors was obvious and reasonable. In other cases, it was rather surprising and unintuitive.

The value of these statistically correlated behaviors is rather simple. Leaders who are already skillful at a given behavior often hit a wall in trying to further improve. Linear development techniques sometimes run out of gas. You can run only so many miles in the same direction and get results. These leaders have already read the book. They've taken the class. They've been to the seminar. Now what? Companion behaviors provide a new and more complete pathway to development.

In order to build trust, I invite you to explore a new path to development using this research-grounded cross-training approach. There are four statistically linked companion behaviors that enable people to be better at expertise:

- Being a role model
- Anticipating problems
- Connecting your work to a vision
- Keeping others informed

As you read through the different enabling behaviors, identify one or two that would be most beneficial in helping you either increase your personal expertise or use the expertise of others to build trust. You will find that people value your expertise, which enables problems to be easily solved. This will help build the trust others have in you.

Be a Role Model

People who rated high on expertise were also rated high on being a role model. Sharing your knowledge is an obvious way of building trust in your expertise with others. The way you share that knowledge is also important. A mentor is supportive and shares information freely, but they are also open to learning new information from others.

They know that expertise flows both ways; you can often learn as much from a mentee as they do from you. In order to create an atmosphere where others share their expertise and knowledge with you, you need to demonstrate that you are reliable, that you will do what you say and say what you do. This is basic training for trust building and has one of the strongest correlations with expertise. It is cyclical.

To improve your ability to be a role model, start by keeping commitments. Take note of the commitments you make to others, and follow through with all of them. People often agree to do something in good faith but forget about it later. Write it down, add it to your calendar, or set an alert on your phone—whatever it takes to keep that commitment.

Ask for feedback—and act on it. Leaders who are able to accept feedback are perceived as role models for their team. Leaders who are able to implement effective changes based on that feedback are exceptional.

Finally, walk the talk. If you say you'll do something, do it. Look for opportunities to be a good example and a role model. Put forth extra effort. Be an example of the behaviors you would like others to demonstrate.

Anticipate Problems

Another way to improve your expertise is to anticipate problems. Research has shown that most people can be quite good at anticipating potential problems. The problem is that we just do not take the time to think about and list what might go wrong or what might become a problem that is not a problem now. We move so quickly to execution that we never take the time or make the effort to consider potential issues. If you take the time to plan, organize, and consider what might go wrong before jumping into action, good results become more likely.

To improve your ability to anticipate problems, you can start by thinking about what could go wrong with your plan. Once you recognize those potential problems, look for how they can be avoided or quickly identified. Monitor your progress, and regularly check whether milestones are achieved. When you are busy executing, it is easy to lose track of the time and the expected completion date. Look for and identify situations where change is needed, and initiate that change early.

The ability to identify critical changes is an essential part of effectively anticipating problems. Finally, look for patterns. Learn to spot new problems and recognize trends. Stay informed through regularly reading and listening to others who are monitoring these trends.

Connect Your Work to a Vision

Working to connect your work to your vision can also improve your expertise. Frequently, the needs and concerns of our situation outweigh the longer-term vision. It is easy to get caught up in solving an immediate problem without thinking about the bigger picture.

Imagine you and your partner have just graduated from college. You have been poor starving students for a long time but now have good-paying jobs. You need a car and feel a strong need to impress your colleagues at work. With the salaries of both you and your spouse, you can easily make the car payments. You choose a high-end, sleek and classic, high-performance two-door import. Within a few years, you have a child and discover that it is almost impossible to get a car seat into the back of the car. As you trade your classy sport model in on an economical minivan, you realize you did not think about the future at all in buying the car.

It is easy to focus on solving an immediate problem, but if you take the time to consider your vision—the direction of the organization— your solution might be very different.

To improve your ability to connect your work to the big-picture direction of the organization, link the vision to individual jobs and everyone's current reality. Help people understand the connection between their individual job, organizational goals and objectives, and the strategic direction of the organization. Take the time to help people understand how their work contributes to broader business objectives and links to the larger strategy. This will let them see how their work directly impacts the bottom line. Fire quickly but only after you have aimed properly. The phrase "Ready, fire, aim" describes a person who is quick to act but not clear about the overall strategy of the organization. Those who act quickly need to be very clear about where they are going and why.

Keep Others Informed

Finally, keeping others informed helps those around us trust our expertise no matter how limited it might be. I did a study where we looked at initial 360-degree assessment results compared with a second assessment done 18 to 24 months later. The data was collected for 4,216 leaders. I was interested in which competency was the easiest to improve. I found that communicating powerfully was number one.

It is not difficult to keep others informed. But when we examined effectiveness ratings for 85,902 leaders, we found that communicating powerfully was rated as number 13 of 16 competencies. Why is something that is easy to do typically not done well? The problem is that most people assume others know what they know. You might think everyone knows what you are working on, but they usually do not have a clue. If you want to make a big splash and show some immediate improvement on an important competency, improve your ability to keep others informed. Create a rhythm to let others know about what you are doing, deadlines that are approaching, expectations from others, and successes that have been achieved.

To further improve your ability to keep others better informed, begin every meeting with an update on the goals and your team's progress on their objectives. Create an open-door policy. Ask your team if they feel they can approach management at any time; if they can't, fix that. Communicate more amid uncertainty. Don't use ambiguity as an excuse to hoard information. Even if you don't know where your path may lead, tell your team where you think it will go and any hidden paths you can imagine. They need to be able to help read the map.

Begin by asking yourself, "What would I want to know or learn more about if I were sitting in the audience?" and "What are their biggest concerns pertaining to this matter?" Be sure to speak to those issues.

Last but certainly not least, establish a communication schedule. Most people fail to communicate important information because they assume others already know or because they wait too long to inform them. Share information regularly and periodically so your teams know when to expect it.

THE LINK BETWEEN EXPERTISE AND JUDGMENT

We trust experts. We have all faced a thorny problem where we did not know which direction to go and then found an expert whose judgment we trusted. We trust the kind of judgment where the person doesn't jump to conclusions and isn't easily swayed by bias, but where their expertise is built through time, study, and experience.

On a sunny day in 1983, at the USSR's missile tracking center, the judgment by a duty officer named Stanislav Petrov saved the lives of millions.[6] The fall of Communism had made relations between the US

---

6 "Soviet Officer Who Averted Nuclear War Dies," Associated Press, September 20, 2017. "The Man Who Saved the World Finally Recognized," Association of World Citizens. Archived from the original on May 21, 2004, retrieved July 29, 2021.

and the Soviet Union even more strained than during the Cold War. One day, Petrov was informed that his satellites had detected a US missile attack. The choice to send the information up to senior ranks was his. He asked his technician how accurate the reading was. One hundred percent accurate. A reading that perfect was unusual, so he decided to wait for corroborating evidence, but none arrived. He went through all the details and considered how strange it would be for the US to strike with just five missiles. The stakes were impossibly high, but he chose to disobey Soviet military protocol and report it as a system malfunction. In a later interview with the Russian BBC's service in 2013, he explained, "I had all the data. If I had sent my report up the chain of command, nobody would have said a word against it."

As it turned out, the false alarms were the result of an uncommon alignment of sunlight on a group of clouds that caused the satellites to mistake them for missiles.

Stanislav had more than a gut feeling that day. He had the experience to know that an accuracy reading that high was too unusual. He had the ability to think through all the information he had received and hadn't received. He had the courage to accept the consequences of reporting and not reporting the incident.

Experts can bring clarity, a path forward, and clear insight. Experts cause the fog to lift and allow people to see the way forward. Experts can help people reduce anxiety and feel a greater sense of hope with the insights they provide. They may not have all the answers, but you can trust in their judgment.

Sir Andrew Likierman, a professor at London Business School, wrote these pivotal words about the power of good judgment: "Leaders need many qualities, but underlying them all is good judgment. Those with ambition but no judgment run out of money. Those with charisma but no judgment lead their followers in the wrong direction. Those with passion but no judgment hurl themselves down the wrong paths. Those with drive but no judgment get up very early to do the wrong things. Sheer luck and factors beyond your control may determine your eventual success, but good judgment will stack the cards in your favor."[7]

7 A. Likierman, "The Elements of Good Judgment: How to Improve Your Decision-Making," *Harvard Business Review*, January–February 2020.

CHAPTER 5

Consistency

In 2017, a video of a United Airlines passenger being forcibly removed from his seat went viral. Customers were outraged and disappointed by the violence and inconsistency in how the flight staff treated that particular customer versus other customers in the plane. The airline's stock dropped 4 percent immediately following the release of the video. That is $1 billion off the market value. Up until this event, there had been normal complaints like any other company receives, but United had been a reliable airline.

Oscar Munoz, chief executive of United Airlines at the time of the viral video, responded awkwardly, initially standing by the choice of the staff on that plane. After receiving more public backlash, United Airlines released a statement reaffirming their dedication to their customers. This did not fix the issue. The public did not know what was true and how they were expected to be treated in the future.

A year later, the company ranked at the bottom among airlines for customer service and scored well below the average on the

2017 American Customer Satisfaction Index for US-based airline companies.

If you treat 30 of your customers fairly and then 3 with bias and cruelty, customers will not know which category they will fall under. Your business will very likely be seen as inconsistent. Even if you complete 10 projects on time but fall behind on the 11th, you will be considered inconsistent.

Although the ratio there is quite small, it is significant. Expertise gets blown out of the water by inconsistency. When your work is not consistent, no one trusts your expertise, and no one trusts you. Throughout my research, most people who get low marks on consistency think that a 1-in-10 ratio is small, but I would argue that it is not. If you have a 10 percent chance of getting your finger cut off with a saw, would you take that chance?

CONSISTENT DATA FOR INCONSISTENCY

I looked at 360-degree assessment results for leaders to understand the impact of low ratings for consistency. I identified those in the bottom 20 percent and examined the results from 20,680 leaders. While these leaders may have had some good traits, their inconsistency generated a negative overall perception of their capabilities. The following is a list of negative consequences that come from inconsistency.

- The leaders' judgment was not trusted in making decisions.

- They were not trusted by their teammates.

- They did not follow through on objectives and tended to get distracted.

- They often failed to achieve agreed-upon goals.

- They resisted taking steps to improve.

- They did not cooperate well with others.

- They failed to anticipate problems until it was too late.

In general, these people seemed to be perceived as not caring about outcomes at work and lackadaisical about their job in general. It seemed that a little bit of inconsistency went a long way, long enough to have a profoundly negative effect on almost every other competency and behavior.

Looking at the data for individual contributors who were in the bottom 20 percent on consistency, I found many of the same items on that list, but I found some additional items that bubbled to the surface:

- They failed to achieve goals in the allotted time.

- They resisted setting high standards of excellence.

- They withheld or forgot important information.

When an individual contributor is inconsistent, their managers and peers start to question their ability and desire to deliver results. Those who were inconsistent also received low performance ratings for both productivity and effort by their managers. They also had low ratings for personal trust and overall effectiveness. Figure 5.1 shows how increased consistency impacts the four different outcomes. Those in the top 20 percent for consistency had all of the outcomes in the 80th percentile or higher.

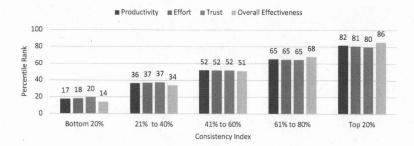

Figure 5.1: Impact of consistency on performance rating, trust, and overall effectiveness.

BUILDING AND IMPROVING CONSISTENCY

Sometimes, leaders want a quick-fix solution, but often, there are a number of very basic activities that can help improve consistency.

You can begin with honesty and empathy. Answer questions truthfully, even if the answer will cause pain. It is better to strain a relationship temporarily than to destroy trust. You should also convey an attitude of concern and caring, especially when imparting bad news. Empathy goes a long way toward establishing trust. When you have to say no, explain why; a rejection may be hard to swallow, but sharing the reasons behind it can build trust. Confront difficult problems directly and promptly. Whenever possible, offer to help someone who is swamped.

Continue with clarity and avoid ambiguity. Acknowledge when you are expressing your own opinion versus fact. Be extremely careful about promising outcomes you cannot control.

You must always walk the talk. Stand up for what you believe, even if it is not the popular position. Don't be afraid to communicate bad news to the person you report to. Keep your boss informed in order to prevent unhappy surprises. Consult with your boss regarding problems before they become disasters. Don't make promises if you are not reasonably certain you can and will keep them.

Finally, commit to the work. Approach your work as if your responsibilities extend beyond your immediate job description. Take an owner's perspective, not just a hired hand's view of the organization. Volunteer for assignments about which you feel enthusiastic. Constantly ask, "Is there a better way to do this?" Commit extra time and effort when the situation calls for it. Propose solutions to problems, even those outside your area, when appropriate.

Additionally, in the same way that there are companion behaviors that naturally increase expertise, there are also companion behaviors that will help improve consistency.

Deliver on Your Commitments

Every time you agree to deliver X product by Y date, you are making a commitment, and the expectation is that you will deliver. When you make that commitment, your supervisor or another stakeholder also makes a commitment with their next-level manager, shareholders, or other parties. Missing your commitment not only hurts you and your reputation but also has a negative impact on the people relying on you, which, in turn, creates more negative feelings toward you. Don't take commitments lightly. If achieving a deadline is a bit of a stretch, then say so.

Another problem with missing commitment targets is the surprise it foists on your manager or the customer. Because we tend to resist confrontation, people are often reluctant to keep others informed about their progress. If a manager asks them for a progress report, they will often say, "I am doing OK," when, in reality, they are in trouble. This all leads to a more negative impression. You are responsible for managing the expectations of others, and your commitments and actions directly create those expectations.

Anne had worked hard to move up in her career and into the executive level. Once she became an executive, she promised herself that she would do whatever was necessary to succeed. After a few days in her new position, she found that a string of people would appear at her door with requests. She felt a bit like the king of the land, with many people wanting both her support and her time.

Soon after being appointed, she found Bob, one of her direct reports, at her door and looking nervous. He asked if he could get her opinion on a technology issue in the organization. After she gave some guidance on the issue, Bob said, "So am I going to be OK in my current position?"

Anne did not know much about what Bob even did or his competence, but in an effort to make him feel better, she said, "Bob, I am sure you are going to be fine."

Bob looked relieved and left her office.

After getting better acquainted with what was happening in her organization, Anne became aware of a significant looming change. Several of the employees would need to be let go for the organization to finance some new equipment. The new equipment would improve efficiency, so the loss of the employees would not negatively impact the group's results. As Anne looked down the names of employees on the list to be laid off, she saw Bob's. She then sighed to herself and said, "I guess Bob is not going to be OK."

No one ever forgets the promises other people make, and too often, we make promises we cannot keep.

Manage Your Commitments

We all want to be the kind of person who is willing to take on additional work, but the inconsistency of not completing a project will have a negative impact that remains with you for a long time.

I worked with a colleague who was an expert on managing this kind of problem. When asked if he could do some additional work, he would always start by saying, "I would love to jump right in and do that project." I always liked hearing his willingness to do the project, but he would then say, "Can you tell me what the priority is for this project compared with all the other projects I am currently working on?" He would then list the other projects that were high-priority projects and say, "Is this more important or less important than those projects?" Often, I would realize the new project was less important than the project he was already working on. By prioritizing his current commitments, he was able to effectively and consistently deliver without overpromising. Most people believe that everybody is aware of how busy they are and exactly what they are working on, but typically, that is not true. Sharing your commitments communicates that information while also indicating the valuable work you do for the company.

There are many actions you can take to improve your ability to deliver on your commitments. First, track them. Write down the commitments that you personally make to other people, and ensure that you follow through. Create a plan that addresses the classic questions of *Why? Who? Where? When? How?* and *How much will it cost?* While every question cannot be addressed, a reasonable amount of detail is required. Once you have created a plan, look for creative, innovative ways to execute it. Creativity can bring life and motivation to a project. Others will hold you accountable for your commitment, so it's best to take personal responsibility for the results of a task, job, or problem that you take on from the start.

Insist on High Standards

It seems counterintuitive to suggest that setting high standards helps you be perceived as more consistent. Although having high standards makes it more difficult to consistently achieve goals, holding yourself to those high standards means you'll work harder to achieve those goals before you share them with others or move on to the next project.

Frequently, when working with teams and committing them to achieve goals, you run into a behavior referred to as *sandbagging*. Sandbagging is where you set a goal exceptionally low so that you are sure you will be able to achieve it. Salespeople are experts at this, but people in many other functions have learned the approach. Excessive sandbagging can also create a negative expectation. It starts to feel as if the people who sandbag don't really want to work hard but, rather, want to set a low bar for minimal performance. If a sandbagger exceeds their goal by too much, then next time, it will be difficult for them to set the goal so low again. People with low standards send the message that they are comfortable with substandard results. Those who set high standards have an interest in doing something exceptionally well.

There is a side effect that comes with high standards. When people achieve a goal that is challenging, their engagement goes up. When they are working at a job that requires little effort, their engagement plummets. When people take on difficult challenges and succeed, it makes them realize that they are competent, capable, and important. And your colleagues' perception of you will go up if you can reach a lofty goal.

Keep your standards high, but of course, make sure they are achievable. Ask others to achieve high levels of performance, and encourage them to perform at their best and always obey the rules. You should establish high standards of excellence for the work your team produces. Begin every staff meeting with a review of the status of the major projects within the group. Get others to help raise the bar. Invite each member of your team to propose two revolutionary goals they would like to see your group pursue.

Continuously Improve

My father had essentially the same job for his entire working life. There were a few changes because of modernization, but he generally did the same work. Today's workers, on the other hand, face continual and sometimes extremely fast changes. Technology evolves much more quickly now than it did in my father's era, and even the nature of work itself is in flux. Clearly, these changes are not slowing down. There is a great deal of data to suggest that, while Generation X workers changed jobs two times in a decade, millennials are expected to change jobs four times in the same amount of time. The pace of change now and in the near future makes the lives of every employee more complicated. Also, as you consider the impact of robotics and artificial intelligence, all employees in the near future will be faced with the need to learn new skills quickly.

Although we can't necessarily predict the exact changes you'll face, change itself is a constant. You can address it by facing it head-on. When you see opportunities for improvement, tactfully share your insights with others. Celebrate small victories rather than waiting for one giant leap in improvement. Set goals that have a reasonable chance of being achieved but that are not so easy as to be empty. Challenge yourself to push a little harder, try a little more, put in additional time, and add extra effort into your work. Look for opportunities to go beyond what is expected of you by not only identifying problems that may not be your direct responsibility but fixing them as well. Determine whether you could exceed in quality or quantity what has been done in the past, then do it.

In the 1980s, W. Edwards Deming helped organizations facing eroding product quality to initiate processes to continuously improve.[8] He created a process called the PDCA cycle, for *plan*, *do*, *check*, and *act*:

- Plan: Identify a personal issue that needs to change, and create a plan.

- Do: Test the plan by putting it into action. Try a new behavior, action, or activity.

- Check: Review the results; analyze what worked well and what did not go well. Summarize what you've learned.

- Act: Take action. With repeated action, execution typically improves. Identify when your actions are effective and when they are not.

---

8   W. Edwards Deming, *Out of the Crisis* (Cambridge, MA: Massachusetts Institute of Technology, Center for Advanced Engineering Study, 1986), 88.

There are a few additional skills that will help you continuously improve. Curiosity helps you ask the difficult questions, imagine what might happen in certain circumstances, and probe possibilities. Curiosity helps you think about new possibilities and solve difficult problems with unique solutions. Another important skill is a thirst for innovation. Rather than being content with using the same old processes, systems, and procedures, the innovator is constantly searching for new and better ways to accomplish their objectives.

Most people believe that they are more consistent than others believe them to be. Others notice when we say we will do something and it does not get done. Sometimes, we don't even remember the promise. Or if we do, we have 10 good excuses that got in the way of us achieving it. Being more conscientious about the promises you make will help you deliver.

BE CONSISTENT ABOUT CONSISTENCY

Remember, the ratio is small but pivotal. One failure in 10 will be seen as inconsistent by your team, your manager, or your customer. To ensure trust from your stakeholders, you have to show them that you can successfully achieve what you say you can 10 out of 10 times. By keeping track of your promises, making reasonable—ambitious but achievable—goals, and seeking improvement at every opportunity, you can reach that level of consistency in anything you do.

CHAPTER 6

Relationships

Larry was my manager. We had a one-on-one meeting once a month. Before each meeting, I wrote down a list of things for Larry to do for me. We would meet up, and Larry would give me a firm handshake and a smile. Then he would thank me for taking the time to meet with him and congratulate me on my accomplishments. After we sat down, he would inquire about my family. It never seemed as though he asked about my family because he felt obligated to do so after reading it in some management book. Instead, it felt sincere, as though he really cared.

Larry would then say, "There are a couple of things I need you to do for me if you have the time." He would give me several assignments and always included the offer to help me in any way with these assignments. He would then express his appreciation for me and all my efforts.

As I left the office, I never once gave Larry the list of things he could do for me. I knew he was busy and had more responsibilities than I had, but I also knew that Larry truly cared about me, and I trusted him completely.

When I considered which of the three pillars was most critical, intuitively I thought that the pillar of demonstrating consistency would be most important. Saying one thing and doing another seems as if it would really hurt trust the most.

Surprisingly, it was relationships that had the most substantial impact. Perhaps the reason that relationships have more impact than consistency is that everyone appears to be a bit inconsistent. We all intend to do things that don't get done and we are not punished too harshly for it in our relationships, but it is actually the very nature of those relationships that appears to be the keystone for trust. Once a relationship is damaged or if it was never created, it is difficult for people to have trust.

If people don't like you, it doesn't matter how consistent you are or how much of an expert you are in any field. They will choose someone they are more comfortable working with.

HOW TO BUILD POSITIVE RELATIONSHIPS

Positive relationships are critical in building trust. Those positive relationships must be developed with sincerity and boundaries. There is not a quick-fix solution, but there are a number of very basic activities that can help in building positive relationships.

Something as simple as how you greet people can be an effective relationship-building tool. Pleasantly greet people when you meet them in the hall. Do not leave others feeling you ignored them; be sure to include everyone.

Demonstrating an interest in people and their work also fosters relationships. Keep yourself informed about what the people in your group are doing. Ask for opinions from your peers and subordinates about new or interesting technologies, theories, work processes, policies, and procedures. Expand conversations to include outside hobbies and interests; people are more than just their jobs.

Time is a valuable commodity, and investing it in your colleagues can greatly improve your relationships. Make yourself available to talk. Show people you have time for them by approaching them and talking informally. Even if you're busy, welcome people who approach you to talk. If they approach you at an inconvenient time, make an appointment to speak to them when you can visit more freely.

Your setting can also be conducive to relationship building. Be available in areas where issues other than work can be freely discussed, such as the lunchroom, parties, and informal activities. Get away from your desk, and wander around the work area. Share information you think will help others. Ask questions about the projects people are working on, and in time, they will reciprocate.

Participate in informal gatherings and events. Don't dismiss the conversations around the water cooler as a waste of time. They are often very efficient mechanisms for sharing information if they are kept to a reasonable length. And don't eat lunch in your office! Use lunch as an opportunity to build relationships and share information.

I have also found in my research that there are separate behaviors that can, if they are developed, enable and build a more substantial behavior. There are four choices that a leader can make that will immediately improve their relationships and secure stronger positive relationships: coaching and developing others, inspiring and motivating others, cooperating rather than competing, and asking for feedback.

Coach and Develop Others

Can you think of a person who has taken you under their wing, coached you, mentored you, or helped you develop? If so, how do you feel about that person? One of the greatest gifts you can give a person is helping them build a new skill. By identifying people who want mentoring, you can build positive relationships. Developing others does not always require you to be the teacher or the coach. You are simply giving others access and encouragement on the job activities or developmental experiences that matter to their careers. This can happen only if you know what others want to do and understand their career goals and plans.

Taking the time to learn about your staff or colleagues is a great starting place for developing others. Other moves you can make in order to develop others include providing one-on-one coaching or mentoring to individual team members or peers. You can schedule career development discussions with each team member; they can be short, but they must be consistent. In one-on-one conversations, set a goal to avoid giving advice. Get comfortable listening and supporting others in discovering their own solutions. Also, set a self-improvement goal for those one-on-one conversations; for example, try to listen more, prepare better questions, or explore three options before making decisions.

Inspire and Motivate Others

Several years ago, I asked my daughters, "What do leaders do?"

They replied, "A leader is the boss. They give orders and tell people what to do."

I then asked where they got those ideas about leaders. They responded, "From you! You are always telling us you are the boss!"

Most people at an early age learn that leaders need to push or drive for results. When we hold others accountable, set deadlines, and provide others with direction, we are driving for results. This ends up being a very important skill and helps accomplish objectives. It is definitely one way to achieve objectives, but it can also backfire: No one wants to be pushed.

There is another way to accomplish objectives. Instead of pushing, you could try pulling your team along with you. Pulling is the ability to inspire and motivate others. Get people excited about accomplishing a goal.

In my research, I discovered that the best leaders do both. They push and pull. A leader who strictly pushes appears to care only about getting the job done, but a leader who knows how to pull helps their team members feel valued and part of something bigger than themselves.

To pull your team up with you, consider bringing positive emotions to work. Frequently convey your own passion and commitment about the work you are doing. Your emotions are extremely contagious. Not only will you pull your team by modeling enthusiasm, but they'll pull each other along with their own increased positivity. Schedule time to listen to your team's concerns and needs. Do not try to solve the concern right that moment; just listen. Involve your team in identifying and adopting a difficult stretch goal. When people accomplish an imposing objective, they are more motivated and engaged. Brainstorm; set aside time every week to have the team bounce ideas off each other and think creatively about business solutions.

Cooperate Rather than Compete with Others

A tenet of Western society is independence: independent work, independent success, and independent failures. Independence allows the individual the opportunity to receive all the credit for accomplishments and all the criticism for mistakes. This way of life simplifies outcomes: No one can take credit for your success, and you are not taking the fall for others.

But this "simplification" is often associated with the framing that the individual is in constant competition with others. The assumption of competition often pushes people to resist building positive relationships with others. It keeps the individual looking inward rather than reaching out.

One solution to this tricky habit of looking at the world through the lens of competition is to realize that there is a huge body of research that concludes that, in most conditions, teams are more productive than individuals. One of the reasons organizations exist is to bring together the efforts of individuals so that synergy is created.

An individual who resists collaborating and cooperating with others is at a great disadvantage in building positive relationships. Make some small, positive steps toward working with others. To improve, begin by looking for opportunities for cross-functional teams to work together. Give recognition and credit to other teams and individuals. Share knowledge and information freely with other groups. Invite other groups or individuals outside your team to attend staff meetings and share their insights and ideas. Find opportunities to help and assist other teams. These specific actions will enhance your entire organization's success while building relationships with other teams.

Ask for Feedback

Most people believe that they are good judges and can discern whether others trust or distrust them. I did a study using people's own self-rating to measure their ability to predict trust. In essence, this study revealed that some people imagine they are very trusted when, in fact, they are not. Additionally, others fear that they are not trusted when they really are. We humans are generally not good at discerning how well other people trust us.

The only way for you to get a good read on your level of trust is to be more open and to ask for more feedback. People who resist feedback are less trusted, but those who are better at asking for feedback are significantly more trusted, which makes them more effective leaders. To put it simply, being more open to feedback and making a habit of asking for feedback can, in and of itself, build trust.

Be aware that when you ask for feedback on an issue of trust, many people will tell you what they think you want to hear. If you ask, "Am I trusted?" the reply you might get is "Absolutely. Everyone trusts you." Some people may be more candid, but the best way to get a good estimate of your trust level is to ask, "What could I do that would help people have greater trust in me?" Another question might be "Are there any actions I have done in the past that caused people to distrust me?" Starting from the assumption that others probably do not have as much trust in you as you think puts you in a frame of mind to uncover—and address—problems.

There are several developmental actions you can take to get more feedback from others. Ask for feedback in a way that shows you really want to improve. Rather than saying, "Was that meeting OK?" ask, "What could I have done in the meeting to significantly improve my performance?" Be specific about what you are requesting feedback on. Identify the right person to give you the feedback you need and the best medium in which to ask. Show gratitude for the feedback you receive, and express your desire for more.

FINDING THE TIME FOR RELATIONSHIPS

As people read through this list of activities, one of their biggest concerns is the amount of time all of this will take. I believe that you can have meaningful and effective conversations that are also brief. Everyone has been in a one-on-one meeting where the other person talked on and on and never came to any conclusion. In order to encourage brief conversations without being rude, let people know how much time you have available to talk. When someone comes into your office and says, "Can I talk to you?" one thing you can do that will help limit the conversation is to say, "Yes, I would love to talk. I have 10 minutes." Often, people will attempt to fit what they have to say into that time period.

You can also set up short meetings so that a time frame is inherent in the meeting from the beginning. It will surprise you how much you can get done in a short amount of time. You should also work to keep the meeting on track. People will often wander off their point, so you may have to pull them back to the topic at hand. Ask them, "What issue are you trying to solve?" or "What's your solution to this problem?" Sometimes, when a person does not seem to have any solution, you can say, "Why not take some time to consider some alternatives? Let's meet tomorrow to discuss." Thank them for their time and willingness to discuss these issues with you, but let them know you have other commitments that require your attention.

RELATIONSHIP BUILDING IN ACTION

Bella was the CFO of a small consultancy that worked remotely, without a permanent office. Working remotely was perfect for Bella, because she had a comfortable home and a perfect office space. She expressed that she was not all that fond of working closely with others, so this situation was a good fit. She liked being independent, and she was extremely competent at her job. She consistently hit every deadline and, because of her experience, was able to identify a variety of new practices and procedures that made the accounting function run more efficiently and provide more accurate forecasts.

After six months on the job, Bella had her first performance review with the CEO. The CEO started with the good news. He complimented her on all that she had been able to accomplish since joining the firm. He said, "You always deliver on your commitments, and your new ideas have done wonders to improve our forecasting." He then hesitated and said, "But," and paused for a few seconds.

Bella grew concerned at this point and said, "But what?"

He said, "A lot of the leadership team have some trust issues with you."

Bella inquired, "You mean they do not trust my forecasts or the accounting totals?"

The CEO replied, "No, they trust the accounting totals, but the new forecasts were much less optimistic for several departments, and the leaders of those groups felt you were out to get them."

Bella replied, "I just looked closely at our pipeline and provided what I thought was an accurate forecast. What am I doing that causes people not to trust me?"

The CEO said, "There are a few things that I have noticed. Would you like to hear them?"

Bella said, "Absolutely."

The CEO then provided Bella with a list of recommended actions that might help her to build trust.

"First, Bella, turn on your camera on Zoom calls."

Bella replied, "I do not like to look at myself on the screen. Most of the time, I am not wearing makeup or I have a baseball cap on my head."

The CEO then said, "No one loves to see their picture on the screen, but when everyone else has their camera on, it feels like you don't care to be part of the group. You need to show that you are present and interested."

He went on, "Second, none of the executive team really knows you. When you have questions, rather than calling them, you send an email. Often, the email interchanges go back and forth several times, and it would have been far easier to have a conversation. Third, many team members feel you do not like them and believe that they are incompetent in their jobs."

Bella replied, "I like them all. I just don't really know them."

Based on the feedback, Bella made a concerted effort to turn on her camera and increase her interaction with each team member. This did take time, and she was not always comfortable, but over time, she found herself developing some close friendships and she looked forward to those interactions. When she called, rather than just asking a question, she took the time to check in with each person and inquire about some personal issues. To better understand her forecasting, she lined up a lunch meeting with team members, which made her forecasts even more accurate.

By the time of her next performance review with the CEO, the news was all positive. The CEO commented, "Bella, I believe that the executive team trusts you more than me."

THE DOWNSIDES OF POSITIVE RELATIONSHIPS

Even though positive relationships significantly impact all other leadership markers for the better, managers are often afraid to prioritize positive relationships with their staff. Questions come up: Is the most loved manager the most effective leader? Is there a downside to having a strong, positive relationship with your team members? Should a manager try to be best friends with their team?

Often in my research, I find that there are two assumptions that people make about why it is best to maintain distance and avoid getting too cozy with their staff. First, if a leader has a close personal relationship with direct reports, they may lose objectivity and avoid giving corrective feedback when needed. The positive relationship will lead to bias and favoritism on the part of the manager. Second, if direct reports have a positive relationship with their manager, they will use that relationship leverage to take advantage of the manager.

It is true that managers can sometimes be biased by friendship and that direct reports can use their relationship to manipulate their manager. This fear of manipulation and bias causes many leaders to intentionally create distance between themselves and their teams. However, these potential detriments are outweighed by the benefits of positive professional relationships.

Several years ago, I was at a presentation by a senior leader in a telecommunication company. The leader started the presentation by saying, "This morning, I asked myself, Have I ever fired someone too soon, or have I waited too long?" He then said, "Because my business had a significant downturn, I have had to fire hundreds of people, but I can't think of one that I fired too soon."

He went on to say, "Most of the time, I waited too long, and that hurt our business, but it also hurt those that I had to fire. They missed taking other job opportunities because I waited too long."

The positive personal relationships this leader had with his employees caused him to put off firing some of them. It also made it more difficult for him personally to let these people go. For most people, having a positive personal relationship with another person makes giving corrective feedback or having to let a person go more difficult.

Nevertheless, I stand with the belief that the benefits of prioritizing positive relationships far outweigh the costs. Those negative effects are not even close to holding a candle to the positive outcomes that come from prioritizing positive relationships.

To analyze the negative effects of positive relationships, I first examined data from 14,014 direct reports who assessed 2,956 managers. I wanted to examine the common assumption that leaders who had positive relationships with direct reports would show favoritism toward some employees and a negative bias toward others.

In order to examine these biases, the managers were rated on the extent to which they had a positive relationship with direct reports, using items such as the manager's ability to balance the pursuit of results with a concern for others' needs, whether the manager was supportive of people from different backgrounds, whether they promoted a spirit of teamwork and cooperation with others, whether they put the needs of the team above their own self-interest, and their level of commitment to helping others succeed. I also asked the direct reports whether they felt they were treated fairly and to what extent. I wanted to know if the leaders who had the most positive relationships got lower ratings for fairness.

Figure 6.1 shows the results. Clearly, the more positive the relationship, the more direct reports felt that they were treated fairly. Evidently, when their leaders had excellent skills at developing relationships, every employee felt that their manager had a positive bias toward them.

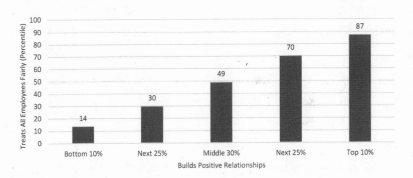

Figure 6.1: Impact of positive relationships on fairness ratings.

I did a second study where I assembled assessments from 467,527 direct reports in a global database of 90,423 leaders. I performed two different analyses. First, I looked at correlations between relationship building and 57 other behaviors to understand whether having positive relationships had negative impacts on any other behavior. I found no negative correlations. In fact, all of the correlations were significantly positive.

I also asked the direct reports how willing they were to go the extra mile in their current job. Many people will work harder and do more for a leader when they have a positive relationship with them. If having a positive relationship has a negative effect on outcomes, it should show up in the results.

The direct reports rated their willingness on the five-point scale. I considered only those who marked 5 as willing to go the extra mile. Those are the employees who are willing to come in early, stay late, and give 120 percent of their energy and effort every day. Note in Figure 6.2 that those leaders rated as having the best relationship also have the highest percentage of direct reports willing to go the extra mile.

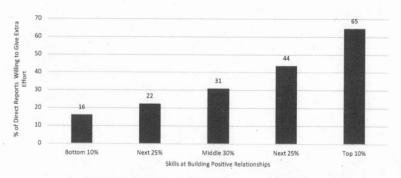

Figure 6.2: Impact of positive relationships on discretionary effort.

In my own experiences over the years and in the studies listed previously, I have found only bits of anecdotal evidence that keeping a distance is positive for leaders. In the vast majority of cases, having a positive relationship only helps a leader be more successful. While there may be some very small downsides to having positive relationships, the upside positives clearly outweigh the negatives.

This research strongly points to positive relationships being the number one biggest factor influencing how much others trust. Improving relationships with others can have a strong positive impact on how much you are trusted, but in addition, it will make your life better in general. If you have ever worked in situations where there was a great deal of conflict at work, you know that your experience added stress and decreased job satisfaction. Finding ways to build more positive relationships will have a strong positive impact on you, how you feel about work, and how much others trust you.

CHAPTER 7

Trust and Inclusion

When my youngest daughter was eight years old, I decided it was time for her to join our family ski crew. I had taught her two older siblings to ski, and even though they had some trauma in the process, I felt confident in my abilities as a skier and teacher to face the mountain with just the two of us.

As we rode the ski lift together and ascended the mountain, she turned to me with a terrified look and asked, "Dad, what if I fall down the mountain and I can't stop?"

I smiled back at her. "Don't worry about it; I'll teach you all you need to know. Do you trust me?"

She thought for a second and replied, "Yes."

She was always my kid who wanted to conquer everything. I gave her some good pointers about what to do, and with a serious and determined look on her face, she quickly took off down the mountain without me. What happened next was a very long fall that some skiers refer to as a "yard sale." Every piece of equipment flew off in various directions, and she lay sprawled on the cold, snowy ground, crying. Fortunately, she was OK, but she looked up at me and said, "Why did I trust you?"

Looking back, I realized my instructional approach was not great, and the hill I put her on was beyond her level. She only agreed to continue skiing if she could learn at ski school. I had lost her trust.

My daughter initially trusted me as a ski instructor only because I was her dad. We often find ourselves in a similar situation, ignoring the subject-matter experts and instead choosing to listen to the person with the most impressive title, the friend of the CEO, or the individual who talks the most. Bryan L. Bonner, a professor at the University of Utah, called these individuals that we place our trust in due to their confidence, extroversion, or position "messy proxies for expertise."[9]

This kind of blind trust relies heavily on our biases—unconscious or conscious. For example, in a study done at NYU, researchers asked a group of diverse participants to rate the trustworthiness of each racially distinct individual shown in a group of photographs. They were instructed to give their "gut reactions" on a scale from one ("not at all trustworthy") to nine ("extremely trustworthy"). The results revealed that unconscious biases dramatically influence the level of trustworthiness toward different social groups in the absence of additional information, despite our conscious desires and intentions.[10]

9 L. Gellman, "Time to Tune Out the Loudmouth," *Wall Street Journal*, September 27, 2013, https://www.wsj.com/articles/BL-ATWORKB-1291.

10 "Psychologists Find Unintentional Racial Biases May Affect Economic and Trust Decisions," NYU, April 25, 2011, https://www.nyu.edu/about/news-publications/news/2011/april/psychologists-find-unintentional-racial-biases-may-affect-economic-and-trust-decisions.html.

Since there are conscious and unconscious biases that influence the initial amount of trust bestowed on a person, does it change over time? What can leaders and organizations do to create high-trust environments that promote diversity, inclusion, and belonging?

There has also been some significant movement around social justice issues. In the last few years, we've seen some organizations take a stand on voting rights and other current issues, while others rejected their employees' urging to speak out. In general, employees desire to work for an organization where they feel included and where there is a strong sense of belonging. This issue is becoming more and more important. Having an inclusive environment needs to move from the C-suite to every manager and supervisor in order for these issues to make a meaningful impact for everyone. Trust is critical for leaders to create that sense of belonging on their team or in their organization.

THE IMPACT OF TRUST AND INCLUSION

To understand the impact of trust and inclusion on effectiveness, I looked at a data set of 2,551 leaders. Each leader had been evaluated on the extent to which they were both trusted and inclusive. I identified those who were in the top 25 percent (476 leaders) and the bottom 25 percent (363 leaders) on both characteristics. I then compared these leaders on 60 behaviors used to identify the most effective and least effective leaders. These two dimensions had a substantial impact on a leader's overall leadership effectiveness. Figure 7.1 shows the dramatic results from leaders in the top and bottom quartile on both trust and inclusion.

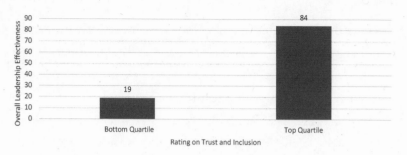

Figure 7.1: Impact of trust and inclusion on overall leadership effectiveness.

This graph shows significant consequences for leaders who ignore or reject their fatal flaws in these two areas. If you are perceived as racist, sexist, two-faced, or dishonest, people are no longer willing to tolerate this behavior. People may have buried or looked beyond these flaws in the past, but the day of reckoning has come. No matter how talented you are, your level of effectiveness depends heavily on your ability to gain trust and include others.

Most people are good and have the desire to help others feel included. The truth is that many don't know how to do it. How do we break barriers and approach uncomfortable conversations? How do we teach people to be more aware of the things they say and do and the things they don't say and do?

A DISCONNECT BETWEEN YOUR BELIEF AND OTHERS' PERCEPTIONS

The vast majority of leaders believe they do a good job of building a climate of trust and openness to the different thoughts, styles, and backgrounds of others. They believe they respect people regardless of ethnicity, race, gender, age, cultural background, or sexual orientation. But often, their colleagues do not agree.

To examine this difference in perception, I gathered 360-degree assessments from 1,825 senior leaders. On average, each leader was assessed by 15 evaluators. Each leader was measured on the extent to which they valued diversity and inclusion. Leaders were also evaluated on behaviors such as creating a climate of trust and openness to different people; respecting people of different ethnicities, races, genders, ages, or sexual orientations; and actively soliciting alternative perspectives. The results from valuing diversity and inclusion were then broken into quartiles based on the assessments of all of the respondents, excluding the leader's self-assessment. The graph below shows the results comparing those self-assessment ratings with the ratings by the leaders' direct reports. Those leaders rated by others to be at the bottom quartile rated themselves at the 42nd percentile on average. In other words, they rated themselves slightly below average. Those rated by others in the top quartile rated themselves slightly higher at the 57th percentile.

Figure 7.2: Self-assessments versus direct report evaluations of valuing diversity and inclusion.

This graph makes a very important point. While the self-ratings of the two groups in the middle are fairly close to the ratings of direct reports, those in the bottom and top quartile are vastly different. The problem is that leaders, in general, think they are doing OK at valuing diversity and inclusion, but in reality, some are very inadequate, and others are excellent, but both are unaware of how others see them.

HOW CAN YOU SHOW OTHERS YOU VALUE DIFFERENCES?

A study by McKinsey showed that US companies spend nearly $8 billion every year on diversity and inclusion training.[11] This sort of sensitivity training gained popularity in the 1980s and '90s and focuses heavily on what not to do or say and on building empathy, but it has missed the mark. In a story circulated in the DE&I (diversity, equity, and inclusion) industry involving an unnamed company, a group of senior white male executives strolled into one such training wearing paper targets that they had personally pinned to their suits for everyone to see.[12] While their actions displayed an evident unawareness of their power and privilege, it also showed the fear that they had of most of the blame in these training sessions being placed on them. Clearly, there is room to improve our ability to value differences and show compassion. These actions did not likely build trust among those leaders' employees.

While there is a lot to unpack in this highly charged topic, I offer just a few best practices based on this research.

---

11 Rick Kirkland and Iris Bohnet, "Focusing on What Works for Workplace Diversity," McKinsey & Company, April 7, 2017, https://www.mckinsey.com/featured-insights/gender-equality/focusing-on-what-works-for-workplace-diversity.

12 Nora Zelevansky, "The Big Business of Unconscious Bias," *New York Times*, November 20, 2019, https://www.nytimes.com/2019/11/20/style/diversity-consultants.html.

Encourage Communication

To demonstrate that you value differences, as a leader, you need to seek out those differences and openly encourage discussion and understanding. Saying nothing doesn't mean that the issues get forgotten or neatly stacked away to be dealt with at a better time; they get worse.

Create a safe environment where people feel they can speak up. Some organizations are fostering communication by creating opportunities to appropriately connect and form better relationships. Others are forming inclusion councils to help them be more proactive and guide their efforts. They are changing meeting structures to include more voices. Efforts such as these take both patience and time, but the increase in communication will help every employee to hear and know that they are valued.

Ask for Feedback

Those leaders who are open to and encourage feedback from others will be much more trusted and inclusive. For example, in a small start-up company, a young male CEO was trying to navigate the issues of communication with his workforce that was growing more diverse. In the past, he had worked with mostly white males, and to put it nicely, there was a lack of awareness and sensitivity to the viewpoints of others. After one company meeting, he pulled aside one of his new female HR executives and expressed his desire to create an inclusive environment. He frankly conveyed to her that he was unsure whether he was a part of the problem and requested that she bluntly inform him of any slipups that could be considered rude or offensive.

She smiled at his request and informed him, "We have a lot of work to do."

Over the next several months, this HR executive felt the courage to bring up small and simple ways to change the language in their organization to be more inclusive and to help others recognize terms that might be interpreted as derogatory. These efforts, initiated by the CEO asking for feedback, set the precedent that every employee was valued.

Too often, we fail to notice our mistakes and inconsistencies, while others see them very clearly. It is like driving without any rearview mirrors: There is much you miss, while others see clearly a broader picture. The simple act of asking for feedback puts you in a position to understand the mistakes you have made, the people you have ignored, and the possibly good things you have done. Leaders who have made the habit of asking for feedback are significantly more effective, simply because others tell them what they need to do to be successful.

Look for Opportunities to Develop Others

Chances are, there have been people in your life who have taken an interest in you, helped shape your career, and influenced your success. Those people occupy a special place in your heart because of this influence they had. If I ask, "How would you describe that person?" the reply is often "a valued colleague," "a great friend," or "an honored teacher." The vast majority of these mentoring relationships occur between people of the same sex, race, and other diversity factors.

The best way to show that you value another person is by finding ways to help them develop. People want opportunities to grow. They notice when the boss picks a favorite or prefers individuals who are of a similar gender, age, or background. The value and impact of support are often underestimated. It may feel passive, but having someone in your corner who trusts and advocates for you can profoundly affect you. This is especially true when contrasted with the opposite situation, where a leader is viewed as looking only for mistakes and expecting subordinates to fail. When you give people opportunities, they feel trusted and included.

I was curious to examine the impact of both high trust and high inclusion to teams. To measure this, I examined data from over 99,000 managers with feedback from only their direct reports. On average, each manager was evaluated by five direct reports. Not only do teams where there is high trust and inclusion have significantly higher levels of engagement (the bottom 10 percent is at the 25th percentile of engagement, and the top 10 percent is at the 71st), but also direct reports were much more likely to be willing to give extra effort (in the bottom 10 percent, only 17 percent of their team members were willing to give extra effort; the top 10 percent had 58 percent willing to go the extra mile). High trust and inclusion make for a powerful combination that can create an exceptional working environment.

WHO DO YOU TRUST?

Accept the reality that you may have biases that you are unaware of. Others, though, see them and feel them. Your job is to assume the best of your team. The world is full of messy proxies for expertise, and the ones you thought might get you down the mountain safely might lead you to fall.

Professor Elizabeth Phelps said, "Whom we trust is not only a reflection of who is trustworthy but also a reflection of who we are."[13] There is trust that is unconsciously given, and there is trust that is earned. Listen, and open your mind to the knowledge and perspectives of others. Everyone, regardless of ethnicity, race, gender, age, cultural background, or sexual orientation, deserves the equal opportunity to be trusted.

13 Damian A. Stanley, Peter Sokol-Hessner, Mahzarin R. Banaji, and Elizabeth A. Phelps, "Implicit Race Attitudes Predict Trustworthiness Judgments and Economic Trust Decisions," *Proceedings of the National Academy of Sciences* 108, no. 19 (May 10, 2011): 7710–5. https://doi.org/10.1073/pnas.1014345108.

CHAPTER 8

Trust and Speed

One afternoon in June, the Wild Boars soccer team and their coach decided to explore some local caves in Thailand.[14] Monsoon season doesn't start until July, and it looked as if conditions were safe. Within hours, things drastically changed: Torrential rains flooded all the trails within the massive cave, and the team was trapped inside. Speed was necessary in finding and getting the boys out as the waters were rapidly rising.

The Thai Navy SEALs, desiring to be heroes for their country, attempted the rescue, but their lack of experience in cave diving, along with choppy waters, forced them back. While others frantically worked pumps to lower the water within the caves, the government's rescue team decided to reach out to two cave rescue experts, John Volanthen and Richard Stanton. When Volanthen and Stanton first arrived, the

---

14 Pat Ralph and James Pasley, "This Timeline Shows Exactly How the Thai Cave Rescue Unfolded," *Business Insider*, June 24, 2019; "Timeline: How the Thai Cave Rescue Unfolded," CNN, July 10, 2018.

conditions in the cave were not good. They knew from experience that with the strong current, any rescue attempt would have to wait.

Trusting in these outside experts must have been difficult for those who wanted immediate action. Other international cave divers also joined the effort, and after nine days, Volanthen and Stanton were able to lay guide lines and found the entire team still alive and safe. But getting them out seemed impossible. The boys had no dive experience, and the journey was difficult for most professionals, due to limited visibility, tight caverns, and strong currents. As they struggled to develop an escape plan over the coming days, oxygen was running out, and they needed to move fast.

Worried that the dive conditions would panic the boys, the divers explained to the Thai rescue officials that the only way they believed they could bring all of the boys out alive, underwater, was to sedate them. The officials were nervous about the operation, but they trusted these divers who had come to help and who proved through their expertise, consistency, and relationship building that they wanted to save the lives of those children. This was the only option.

After 19 days of being trapped and the efforts of hundreds of volunteers and worldwide professionals, all 12 boys and their coach were successfully transported out of the cave. While some trust is built over time, the speed that comes from trust makes impossible things possible.

In 2017, Jack Zenger and I wrote a book called *Speed*. In this book, we discovered the impact of speed on a leader's effectiveness. We found that leaders who were rated in the 75th percentile for speed were also rated as being twice as effective overall, had more engaged employees, and received more positive performance ratings. Leaders who moved more quickly were significantly more effective.

Since we had an excellent measure of both trust and speed, I thought it would be interesting to look at the interaction of these two dimensions with data from a large number of leaders across the globe. Figure 8.1 shows the results. The leaders who were the least trusted (the 1st through the 9th percentiles) had a speed rating in the 22nd percentile, while those who were most trusted (the 90th to 100th percentiles) had speed ratings in the 79th percentile.

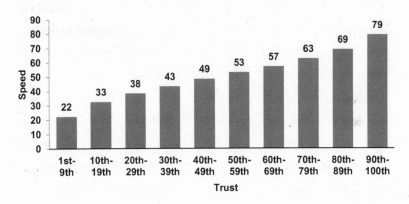

Figure 8.1: Impact of increased trust on evaluations of speed.

It is clear from this data that leaders who were the most trusted were also rated as moving faster.

THE SPEED BUMPS THAT ERODE TRUST

Several years ago, when my children were younger, the city put speed bumps on the road running in front of my house. It was nice, because the speed bumps really worked. Every car slowed down, and many cars avoided the road altogether, finding another route without speed bumps. But the speed bumps are now a frustration to me every time I go down that street because I have to slow down. I worry that if I don't, my car might fall apart.

A variety of issues can erode speed and trust within an organization.

I gathered data from two senior groups of leaders, where they had low ratings for trust and speed. Group A scored in the 20th percentile for trust and in the 32nd percentile for speed. They also had a very low employee engagement rating, in the 6th percentile. Group B, on the other hand, was in the 30th percentile for trust and the 55th percentile for speed and was rated with an employee engagement level in the 25th percentile.

Trust was rated among the most negative issues in both organizations. Looking over the list of negative items, there was a striking similarity between the two lists. It became clear that in order for trust and speed to flourish, there were some behaviors that needed to be addressed.

I identified seven speed bumps that damage trust. These speed bumps create tension, friction, and disengagement in an organization. Taking out the speed bumps will have a significant impact on increasing both speed and trust.

Resisting Feedback from Others

Have you ever done something stupid and then looked around to see if anyone else noticed? When I'm traveling, I sometimes slip into strange accents when speaking with foreigners. I often don't realize I'm doing it. Even though it is a stupid thing, somehow, if only a cab driver or the hotel employees notice, you start to believe it's not a problem, although my family becomes quite embarrassed by my slipups.

I had a colleague who loved to chat about his personal life during meetings. Out of fear of hearing one of his tangents, we would try launching into an agenda quickly to avoid small talk. His constant digressions were a problem, and he wasn't catching the hints. While talking too much about outside things during meetings might seem like a small thing, when this colleague received direct feedback, he made changes, and our meetings were more effective and shorter, and all of our relationships were stronger.

Many of us resist asking for or being open to feedback from others. Usually, that feedback helps you know that you are doing something stupid, and your stupidity has two significant impacts. It slows the organization down, and it erodes trust. I give a lot of presentations, and occasionally, there is a small typo in the text. It always amazes me how one little typo can create a significant negative impression for some executives. Because of that, I have developed the habit of always asking others to review my presentations and papers before they are submitted.

Each of these stupidities may seem inconsequential, but they can have significant effects on others' trust and their impression of you.

Allowing Conflict to Fester

If you fail to clean and cover a cut, it begins to fester. Over time, a serious infection can start to form. Have you ever worked in an organization where there was a great deal of conflict? That situation makes coming to work difficult, and engagement inevitably decreases. Conflict creates friction that slows down everything, and trust suffers.

Imagine yourself in an organization where a new approach is suggested. Rather than testing out the new approach, it is critically debated and evaluated. In the debate, you realize that what is being debated has more to do with who suggested the approach than whether the approach is useful. Conflict inevitably creates winners and losers instead of the free flow of ideas. These kinds of interactions not only erode trust but also slow down progress.

Many leaders assume that their team members should be able to resolve their own conflicts, but that rarely happens. Instead, you should face conflict head-on and defuse it immediately. Finding an amicable solution can often build stronger relationships and enhance trust as the parties move beyond their conflict. Insisting that conflicts are resolved helps the organizational climate improve and increases speed and trust.

Forcing People to Deliver Results

A demand or insistence is often the easiest way to get difficult things done, but no one likes to be compelled. There needs to be an inspiring reason for people to do something difficult. People need a leader who helps them understand their purpose.

During World War II, the German forces were losing their air battle with England. Hitler then shifted tactics. If they couldn't bomb England, they would starve them out by cutting off their supplies. The German U-boats were extremely effective at sinking the Allied ships, and long-wavelength radar was useless for defending against them. The Allies reached a critical point when Britain's oil supply became so low that they were running on fumes. The Allied forces had to find a way to protect those ships. This meant fixing the radar problem.

The United States appointed the eccentric investment banker Alfred Lee Loomis to assemble a team of engineers and physicists to develop a radar system using short wavelengths. With a deadline that meant life or death, Loomis inspired his team to work quickly and collaborate with British scientists to jump-start their efforts. In less than 30 months, the team successfully delivered the first microwave radar device.

However, the system had too many buttons and was difficult for pilots to navigate in these stressful situations. The pilots couldn't successfully use what these scientists had made. They didn't trust it.

When the team of engineers finally understood the needs of these pilots, they didn't push back on what they had created; they knew their purpose was to deliver something that could be effectively used to protect the ships. So they went back and designed it as a grid of pulsed signals covering the Atlantic. This allowed a pilot to easily calculate his location on the grid without being detected.

In the first month of its use, the Allies sunk 41 U-boats, which was more than in the first three years of war. Loomis found a way to rally different groups of professionals to achieve exceptional results.[15]

An Inability to Adapt to a Different Situation

The psychologist Abraham Maslow once said, "I suppose it is tempting, if the only tool you have is a hammer, to treat everything as if it were a nail."[16] Some people have a preferred approach, and since they like it, they apply the same approach to vastly different situations. Today, leaders need to be agile and flexible in their approaches. They need to look at different situations and ask the question, "What approach would work best in this situation?"

In 2019, my son-in-law's main priority at the large health system where he worked was to convince doctors to adopt a telehealth

---

15 Safi Bahcall, *Loonshots* (New York: St. Martin's Griffin, 2019).

16 Abraham Maslow, *The Psychology of Science: A Reconnaissance* (New York: HarperCollins, 1966).

solution for their patients. In one conversation with a doctor who was a few years from retirement, when he presented the system's telehealth option, the doctor responded, "I don't like it. I won't do it. My patients won't like it, so when I am gone, you can come talk to the next guy."

Before the coronavirus pandemic, less than 1 percent of physician visits were conducted via telehealth. In the days following the COVID-19 public health emergency, my son-in-law was rapidly onboarding doctors and training them in telehealth. Due to the shutdown and the lack of knowledge about the virus, physicians had to find a way to keep patients and themselves safe. The crisis forced them to adapt to the new and different mode of delivering care.

In my research on agility, I found that, to be agile, a person needs to start by being open to learning and listening by respecting the opinions of others. An agile person also needs to be willing to stretch and try different approaches. Even the resistant doctor, who had initially refused to come on board, changed his tune. This doctor's practice not only used telehealth but also excelled in it.

That 1 percent changed to 85 percent in just a few months. People can adapt. New behaviors are sometimes difficult to learn, and our first attempts may be awkward, but over time, a new skill can be learned. It helps if a person is optimistic about their ability to learn new skills. And finally, people need to be honest with themselves about their performance.

A Culture That Is Not Open to Debate

Difficult changes require discussion. Without discussion, people walk away angry. Leaders will often assume that an issue has been discussed, but many people are still frustrated.

Anesa Parker, Carmen Medina, and Elizabeth Schill wrote in their *Rotman Management* article "Diversity's New Frontier: Diversity of Thought" that we need to abandon "the idea that consensus is an end in and of itself. In a well-run, diverse team, substantive disagreements do not need to become personal: Ideas either have merit and [points] of connection or they do not."[17]

Being open to debate does not mean that difficult decisions will change, but it allows others to feel heard. Leaders should consider how they can create an environment in which people can disagree and express how they really feel. This kind of thing takes some time and requires some patience, but the lack of opportunity to discuss and debate creates friction about movement and causes some people to want to sabotage a new approach or change.

Ignoring Individual Impact

Several years ago, I had been in Europe for two weeks, working in a variety of different countries. Because of the late nights, international flights, and poor internet connections, I was not caught up on my email. As I returned to the office, I was desperate to get some help on a project from one of our employees. I assumed that they would be in the office when I arrived in the morning, but they were not at their desk. By noon, I was getting more and more anxious, so I went to a colleague and expressed my frustration, only to hear, "Don't you know what happened?"

The obvious answer was "No, I don't have a clue."

All too often, a negative or tragic event happens to an individual

---

17 A. Parker, C. Medina, and E. Schill, "Diversity's New Frontier: Diversity of Thought," *Rotman Management* magazine, Fall 2017.

in the organization. This event grabs the attention of the majority of employees, but you are completely unaware. Most people have heard about this event through the grapevine, but your grapevine has been cut. Because of your lack of awareness, you conduct business as usual, which for all who observe seems insensitive and callous. Compare that situation to one in which you are quickly informed about the negative event, you step in quickly and give this person some support and time off to cope with the situation. What you have done makes the employee with problems feel valued and makes everyone else proud to work for this kind of organization.

In the ongoing stream of growing, delivering, and running successful businesses, leaders can often look past or stay uninformed about their most important asset: their employees.

Alyssa Mastromonaco, former White House deputy chief of staff for President Obama, has had an impressive career but is also aware of her limitations. When she was switching to a new antidepressant medication, she said, "I told the CEO that I was on Zoloft and was transitioning to Wellbutrin. I can react strongly to meds, so I was worried switching would shift my mood and wanted her to know why. I talked about it like it was the most normal thing in the world—it is!" Her boss was completely supportive. While this powerhouse woman brings a load of talent to her job, she also comes with her anxiety.[18]

Trust is built when people know their leaders and the organization have their back—when they can bring their whole self, even the broken parts, to work and they know it's OK.

---

18 Morra Aarons-Mele, "We Need to Talk More about Work," *Harvard Business Review*, 2018.

Working Independently and Avoiding Collaboration

My colleague Jack Zenger and I have worked together for over two decades. We have written eight books together and created hundreds of articles. Our approach has been to create a first draft of a chapter or an article alone and then send it to the other person for edits, changes, and revisions. Most of the time we agree on conclusions, but occasionally we disagree. My first reaction when Jack disagrees or has a different opinion on a topic is often negative. I say to myself, "He can't be right. How could he possibly disagree?" Lucky for me, I say nothing, but I think about his difference of opinion, and after a while, I start to see his point of view. He is not always right, but his pushback always makes what we create much better.

Many people have a preference to work independently and avoid collaborating with others. The problem is that for most work, what you do impacts what others do. When you work independently, you lose the perspective of how what you do affects the work of others. Anytime you create more work and frustration for others, you lose trust. Those who make a concerted effort to involve others will see a big payoff regarding overall efficiency.

THE SPEED OF TRUST

Stephen M. R. Covey claimed in his book *The Speed of Trust* that "nothing is as fast as the speed of trust,"[19] and from my research, I would agree. Trust makes challenging decisions easier. Trust makes adopting new processes and procedures faster. Trust makes

---

19 Stephen M. R. Covey and Rebecca R. Merrill, *The Speed of Trust: The One Thing That Changes Everything* (FranklinCovey, 2006).

collaboration among team members smoother. If you're going to devote a third of your life to your job, then it is worth it to focus on the one trait that will significantly increase your speed.

CHAPTER 9

Trust and Employee Engagement

Anna was a likable leader. She managed a small team of marketing professionals. She was friendly and fun, but she also knew how to push people to get things done. Then Anna had a sour experience with one of her team members, Michelle. Anna received an email from Michelle that caused her to react very negatively. In her frustration, she wanted to forward the email to a friend, along with her commentary saying, "Do you see from this email why I am so frustrated at work!" But then, she noticed that instead of forwarding the email, she replied directly to Michelle. Anna got caught saying one thing and doing another, and that started to erode the trust Michelle had in her. As Anna continually brushed the incidents aside that dealt with Michelle's inconsistency, the tension got worse. Anna had a great team. Surely, a sour relationship with just one member couldn't derail the progress of everyone. Right?

To demonstrate the relationship between trust and engagement, I compiled a data set of 97,632 managers' 360-degree feedback reports. The managers were assessed on trust by their direct reports, and then the direct reports were assessed on their level of employee engagement. Their engagement measured the confidence the direct reports had in achieving the team's or organization's goals, their willingness to go the extra mile, their willingness to recommend the organization to potential new applicants or customers, their commitment to stay with the organization, and their overall satisfaction.

Figure 9.1 shows the relationship between the level of trust of a manager and their direct reports' employee engagement. It is very clear from this study that every incremental improvement in trust drives up employee engagement. On average, each manager was rated by five direct reports.

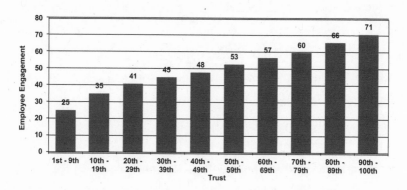

Figure 9.1: Impact of trust on employee engagement of direct reports.

But there is more, and this is the exciting part of the data. What happens when even one person on your team doesn't like or trust you?

Trust is often challenging to build with every team member. Often, leaders relate better to some team members than others. A few team members may require some disciplinary action when they act inappropriately. You may find yourself with a team member you feel distrusts you. If you have one negative team member, this can (on average) lower your scores, but if you do the math, one out of six should not have a devastating negative impact. In my experience, most managers lay all the blame on that one person who they feel is negative.

To study this phenomenon, I looked at individual ratings from 60,438 direct reports completing 360-degree assessments. I identified managers where no team members were rated negatively and others where just one team member indicated their trust needed significant improvement or some improvement. I looked at their overall ratings for trust and engagement from all of their direct reports. What I found was surprising. Having just one team member indicate that trust needed to be improved lowered the trust rating by 31 percentile points and the engagement rating by 14 percentile points!

Figure 9.2 shows the huge shift with lower trust ratings from zero to just one direct report.

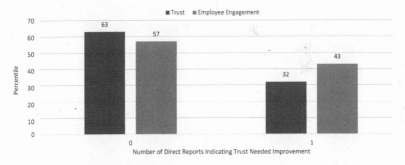

Figure 9.2: Impact of the number of direct reports recommending improvement on trust and engagement scores.

In previous research, I found that ratings of trust tend to trickle up and down. Think about a situation where you are looking to purchase a car. For dealership A, you read all the ratings and reviews and do not find any negative reviews. You find the overall average rating for dealership B higher, but there is one very negative review. That one review can cause you to discount the more positive overall rating. Trust is contagious. When some people trust you, others follow, but it causes others to wonder if their trust was misplaced if someone distrusts you.

After Anna inadvertently sent Michelle that very negative email, she called her boss and asked her for some advice about what to do. Her boss said, "Go to Michelle and apologize, ask for forgiveness, but then help her to understand your frustration and then listen to her about her frustrations with you. Avoid being defensive. Just listen and learn."

For Anna, this was an incredibly difficult encounter, but it provided the opportunity for both people to get their frustrations out on the table. Anna's relationship with Michelle did improve. One thing that Anna learned in the encounter was that the job Michelle had did not fit her skills or her passion. Several months later, another job opened up in the company, and Michelle transferred.

Consider the potential negative impact of low trust, even from just one member of your team. Too often, managers discount the possible adverse effects that only one team member can have. Like Anna, they rationalize that it's just a Michelle problem. What they may not see is that the feelings Michelle is experiencing can spread to other team members. The problem is, if one person distrusts you, it causes others to question and look for something they may have overlooked. Distrust can have a significant negative impact.

If you have a team member who distrusts you, take this very seriously and do everything you can to find a resolution. Talk to them, identify their concerns, and work to improve the relationship. The engagement of your team depends on it.

CHAPTER 10

Trust and Age

We often hear sayings like "With age comes wisdom" and that you should "respect your elders." Many people believe that older leaders, with all this wisdom and respect, are more trustworthy than younger ones. I have measured trust for more than 15 years, and I thought it would be interesting to look at trust as a function of age and time. Before 2015, there was not a clear trend for any age group of leaders being more trusted. However, from 2015 onward, I noticed a clear trend that younger leaders (those 40 and younger) had significantly higher trust scores than the 41-to-50 and the 51-and-up groups. In the last five years, there has been a significant impact from technology and industry disruption that has had a profound impact on many organizations and the way that leaders are viewed.

Figure 10.1 shows the results for leaders who were assessed from 2015 to 2019. For the most part, these are different leaders being assessed. Sixty-five percent of the population of leaders come from the United States, but the remainder are from across the globe. The assessment that collected the trust data was the Extraordinary Leader

360-degree assessment, where managers, peers, direct reports, and others provide feedback to a specific leader.

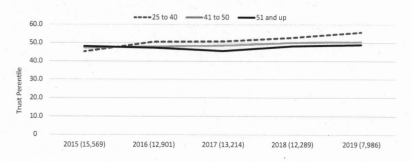

Figure 10.1: Trust in younger leaders increases from 2015 on.

Perhaps we imagine the more youthful person as being erratic or trying unproven approaches, whereas the older person is more stable and consistent. However, the data showed that younger leaders have significantly higher effectiveness ratings for trust that dissipate as they age.

Several years ago, my wife and I traveled to Europe. As on many of our trips together, I combined sightseeing with some work. We started the trip in the United Kingdom, and I can still remember my wife admiring a carved stone flower pot. She desperately wanted it. It was large and heavy, but it fit in my suitcase.

We then went on to Denmark, Germany, and the Netherlands and continued collecting. Toward the end of our journey, it was a real challenge lugging the bags around. In Germany, we almost missed a train because the heavy bags slowed us down. By the time we visited our last destination, my bag was significantly overstuffed. I was afraid that the airlines would not check the bag, but because I was a frequent flyer, they took the bag anyway, and we made it back to the United States.

As I think about this study's results—that as we age, trust declines—I believe it is because we continue to carry some excess baggage. Bad habits, failure to keep up with new technologies, biases, grudges, and impatience are baggage that comes with age. Remind yourself to throw out your excess old baggage. Reinvent yourself, and continue to build trust.

TOP MANAGEMENT OR SUPERVISORS?

When I examined trust as a function of the leader's level in the organization, there was an evident trend that I hadn't expected (see Figure 10.2). The higher one goes in an organization, the lower the trust they receive from the rest of the organization. Even though the absolute differences are not huge, the difference between trust for supervisors and for those in top and senior management positions is statistically significant. Most top and senior managers would argue that their role in the organization requires them to make unpopular decisions that erode the trust that others have for them. At the same time, the top and senior managers also make very popular decisions that could be seen as building the trust of others.

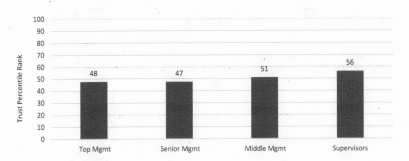

Figure 10.2: As management level increases, trust decreases.

As you look at these demographic trends, remember that trust is not lower for every top and senior manager. Some top-level managers have the highest level of trust. It is not your position that diminishes trust; it is how you behave in the position.

BEWARE OF DIMINISHING TRUST

These trends left me a little perplexed. Why is trust decreasing with age and position? Could it be that the further individuals climb up the corporate ladder, the more distant they become to their direct reports? The once small team that had daily interactions is now a hundred different employees working in different areas. Since trust is built upon three areas—expertise, consistency, and positive relationships—which ones are falling short? You need all three for trust to be strong. When I looked at the numbers, I observed that while expertise stayed consistent or improved with age, there was a steady decline in building relationships and consistency.

Trust isn't established once and then kept forever. It takes consistent work. You can't nurture a plant for one year and then expect it to thrive on its own every year after that. And there are things to learn from these vibrant younger leaders about establishing a firm foundation of trust. The results from this study pointed out the four influential factors employed so well by our younger generations.

A Willingness to Ask for Feedback and Improve

Younger leaders were rated significantly higher for their willingness to ask for feedback from others and to create an atmosphere of continuous improvement. Our research shows that as people age, their willingness to ask and effectiveness at asking for feedback decline. They assume that they have learned all the lessons and have the experience needed to be successful because they did ask for feedback at a younger age. In reality, with the dynamic changes occurring in technology, the needs of every organization are continually changing, which requires leaders to be more agile today. For older leaders to maintain the respect and trust of their teams, they need to ask for and be open to feedback and to continuously look for ways to improve.

Consistency

Younger leaders were rated significantly higher for their ability to be counted on to follow through on their commitments. Too often, older leaders write checks that others cannot cash. Older leaders often tell their team members they are doing fine when the team's performance is only average. They agree to achieve a difficult commitment but then miss deadlines and expect others to accept their excuses. Older leaders are rated lower for their inconsistent ability to honor obligations and keep their promises. This erodes trust.

Building Positive Relationships

Older leaders were rated less positively for a series of behaviors that were all focused on relationships with others. These behaviors included cooperation, collaboration across groups, staying in touch with others' concerns, resolving conflict, skillful communications, inspiring others, and balancing getting results with a concern for others' needs. The bottom line is that we trust those who are more likable. Some people, as they age, seem less willing to invest time and effort to maintain positive relationships, eventually becoming grumpy old men and women.

Poor Judgment and a Lack of Expertise

We trust others who are well informed, who show themselves to be knowledgeable, and who understand new technologies. If a doctor tells you to change your eating habits or give up smoking, it carries more weight than the hundreds of times we've heard this advice from others. When a leader does not have in-depth expertise but is a leader only because of their position, they might make a poor decision and lose the trust of their direct reports or upper leadership. Leaders can gain the perception of expertise by listening to and utilizing the advice of experts in their decision making, which enhances the trust that others have in them.

NOT EVERY OLDER LEADER IS UNTRUSTED

Many of the most trusted leaders are older. It is not a leader's age that causes them to be trusted or untrusted; it is their actions. By being open to feedback, being consistent, having positive relationships, and exercising good judgment, you can become more trusted. Time is something that grows more precious with age. You have only so much time, and it seems to slip away faster every year. I know this and feel it in my own life. Developing trust is an investment of time, and conceivably, some older leaders hesitate to make a deeper investment. My advice to the older generations is to carefully observe the actions of these younger leaders who are building high levels of trust. To the younger generations, I would advise that you keep trusting your elders. They may be a bit more grumpy, but they still care deeply and have a lot to offer.

CHAPTER 11

Trust and the COVID-19 Pandemic

Sir Winston Churchill is credited with saying, "Never let a good crisis go to waste," toward the end of World War II. The COVID-19 pandemic provided a unique setting to study leaders and trust. In March of 2020, most office workers were told to go home, set up their own office, and continue working. Within a few weeks, thousands of people found themselves working from home. Supervisors and managers who had been interacting with their direct reports on a daily basis replaced meetings in the conference room with meetings on various virtual conference platforms. During this period, I continued to gather assessments on leaders with feedback from their direct reports. In June, I had data on more than 1,000 leaders and compared these results with data gathered before the pandemic on 100,000 leaders. With all the chaos that had occurred during the pandemic, I assumed that the effectiveness ratings for the managers would be less positive and their trust ratings would go down. Looking at the data, I was surprised to find that the direct reports' ratings of overall leadership effectiveness improved by 2 percentile points, and trust improved by 3 percentile points. While these differences were not huge, they were statistically significant and unexpected.

Digging into the data on trust, I found that all three factors that had the most impact on trust—the trifecta—showed some improvement during the pandemic, but the results for relationships did not indicate a significant improvement in the initial part of the shutdown. That made sense, given that the vast majority of direct reports were now working remotely from their managers. The separation created by working at home would certainly have some impact on relationships. Consistency and expertise both showed significant improvement in the early part of the pandemic, however.

In this initial period, organizations needed to make a variety of significant changes quickly and efficiently. I looked further into my data and isolated those leaders who had above-average trust ratings to understand what behaviors in the beginning of the pandemic helped them to be viewed as more trusted. This information may be helpful to understand what leaders needed to do in a crisis to increase their level of trust. The analysis of the data identified five capabilities that helped build trust in a crisis.

Expertise and Good Judgment

In a crisis, having a knowledgeable expert is a great advantage, as opposed to an uninformed figurehead leader making decisions with no insight. During the pandemic, a great number of decisions needed to be made quickly. What technology will be needed, how often do we need to meet, how do we share information, what equipment do people need to maintain productivity, and how can we support each other? Leaders who quickly became knowledgeable about important issues and then identified others who had additional expertise were viewed in a more positive way by their direct reports. Leaders who demanded that they control decisions with no knowledge or insight were not trusted.

While some organizations suffered financial losses in the pandemic, others became more profitable. For two of my clients, the pandemic created significant increases in business. One organization was in the packaged food business, and the other was providing building supplies. The challenge for both of these businesses was that while some workers were able to work from home, other workers needed to be in the plants and factories. It was crucial that those workers who were required to come in saw some top-level managers there as well. Both companies dug in deeply to understand what they could do to ensure the safety of their employees, including masking, social distancing, regular testing, and bonus pay. They went through the pandemic with very few problems and came through with a loyal workforce.

Taking Initiative

Succeeding in the pandemic required that leaders follow a completely new playbook and take on tasks they had never done before. Completely changing the way that people in an organization work together is a huge undertaking, and the leaders who were energized and excited to take on new, challenging goals built trust in themselves and the organization.

Those people who were willing to go above and beyond the normal process built additional trust in others. Those who resisted building new skills and taking on additional tasks were less trusted.

Paul is the CEO of a digital consulting firm. This firm was unique because employees had always worked remotely, so when most offices closed, for them it was just business as usual. In order to build relationships and generate morale, Paul's firm had always had an elaborate holiday party, but having an in-person celebration in December 2020 was out of the question. Paul knew they needed to do something, so he went to work and created a plan. He contacted a restaurant that was owned and run by the wife of one of his employees and that was in desperate need of additional business. They discussed home delivery of delicious meals on the day of the party. Paul hired a comedian who knew how to work remotely and interact with his staff to do an event. He had a special present delivered to every employee right before the party. At the end of the party, most employees commented that this was the best party ever.

Consistency

As people moved to working from home, there was a great deal of anxiety. Some employees worried about their future employment and their ability to learn the new skills required in remote work. Having a leader who honored their commitments and kept promises played a critical role in enhancing trust. Those leaders who failed to walk the talk automatically lost trust.

The pandemic was an economic hardship for many, and it was difficult to see large numbers of people suffering. Many CEOs who knew that a significant number of their employees would be out of work also took significant pay cuts. Eric Artz of REI stopped taking a salary, along with Geoff Ballotti of Wyndham Hotels and Resorts, Ed Bastian of Delta Airlines, Brian Chesky of Airbnb, Larry Culp of GE, Michelle Gass of Kohl's, Jeff Gennette of Macy's, Logan Green of Lyft, Mark Hoplamazian of Hyatt, Danny Meyer of Union Square Hospitality Group, Arne Sorenson of Marriott, among many others. Much of the goodwill this generated initially was diminished by some who actually had their total compensation increase because of stock options and bonus incentives, but the initial sentiment was right. By sacrificing along with their workers, these leaders were able to build trust during a difficult time for all of them.

External Perspective and Information

When people are involved in an accident, their perceptual field tends to narrow. They tend to focus in rather than out. In a crisis, that can happen to leaders, but in this crisis, what employees needed was a leader who was constantly focused on a variety of relevant information from outside the organization that would benefit the group. Because working remotely completely changed how many jobs needed to be done efficiently, the best leaders were searching for insights on technology and approaches that would help them and their team members be more effective.

As the pandemic began and offices were closed, many organizations tried to keep their typical cadence of meetings and communications, only to find that an eight-hour meeting on Zoom would just not work. For people to function effectively, there would need to be shorter, more frequent communications. Similarly, our typical training was a one-day, in-person workshop. We found that the most effective live-online format was to move to a 2-hour session on one day and a 2.5-hour meeting the following day. After a scheduling mix-up canceled one of my day-two meetings that got rescheduled to the following week, I found that, for some clients, having a week between sessions was ideal.

Taking the Long Strategic View

The pandemic had a significant impact on organizational plans, objectives, and strategies. Those leaders who took the long view, embracing their current circumstances and then aligning them with the long-term objectives, were able to keep their team on a path that led to success. Overreacting to the crisis caused many employees to lose faith and distrust their leaders.

Before the pandemic, I would generally travel every week. In late February 2020, my wife and I spent 10 days in Australia. I was working and speaking, and she was enjoying Australia. Right after we returned home, we went into lockdown. I had just started a project with a large company in France, and work that I had previously done through travel had to be done through Zoom or Teams. That was a huge learning experience.

Since then, I have been stuck at home, for the most part. While I sometimes miss the good old days of airports and hotels, what has become clear is the productivity increase I have experienced over the last 18 months. Some days, I am doing a session with people in the United States, Amsterdam, and Switzerland, followed by another call with Italy in the late morning, a meeting with a client in Arizona in the afternoon, and in the evening an event with top-level leaders in Vietnam—all from my home office.

I am anxious to be with others in person. The in-person experience is amazing, but when I take the long view, I realize how beneficial the digital experience has been and will continue to be in my work.

Recently, I did a survey for a large group in Washington, DC, and asked a survey question of how many people wanted to go back to being full time in the office. Only 7 percent wanted to go back. The pandemic has changed organizations, and it is highly unlikely that we will go back completely to the way we were working in 2019. What is the long view for your organization? What can you do to capitalize on what happened in the pandemic?

We continued to gather data on leaders during the pandemic, and by the end of 2020 we discovered that trust had improved 5 points and relationships had improved 3 points, with expertise improving 4 points along with consistency. A big surprise from almost everyone in the pandemic is that employee engagement, which was predicted to go down, actually showed a significant improvement. It turns out that most employees enjoyed working from home, and many employers are considering hybrid options when work returns to normal, where some people continue working from home at least part of the workweek.

For some employees who are introverts, remote work became their paradise. They loved the independence and did not miss those awkward interactions they had with their manager and other colleagues. But their paradise was occasionally spoiled because of the unwelcome Zoom and Teams calls, where everyone was required to have their camera turned on. Some made excuses and occasionally turned their camera off. This behavior can cause a loss of trust. Like it or hate it, if you want to be trusted, turning your camera on is critical because it shows that you are present and interested as opposed to lurking in the shadows. Over time, people get used to interacting while on camera, but it does take some time and persistence.

The research on remote work suggests that, for many but not all organizations, productivity is higher. For many employees, their personal productivity is also higher. But there is data that people who work remotely are less likely to be promoted, and it is possible that trust is lower for some remote workers. Once again, considering the trifecta of trust, to increase trust, sharing expertise is always important, consistently delivering what was promised needs to always occur, and your relationships must be strong. Poor performance on any one of these three issues diminishes trust.

CHAPTER 12

Trust and Teams

I t's clear from all the data that trust is contagious. Having a team member who trusts you influences you to trust them in turn. But having a team member who distrusts you also influences you to distrust them right back. As I assess teams, I encounter teams where trust is high and others where trust is low. It is often a surprise to many in the team when trust is low. Individuals know that they distrust others, but they rarely realize that others distrust them too. That lack of trust in the team creates negative engagement with team members. On teams with below-average trust, 64 percent of the team members are thinking about quitting, and only 19 percent are willing to put extra effort into their work.

Let's look at how the trifecta of trust influences teams.

Expertise and Execution

Teams need to be able to solve problems quickly and be knowledgeable enough to make the tough calls and decisions required to operate effectively. Each team member should feel accountable for accomplishing their part of the work. A team needs to be confident in each other that team members will do everything possible to achieve goals and objectives on time and within budget.

Consistency

Unethical behavior is not tolerated in high-trust teams, and team members should insist on honest dealings with one another. A team with high consistency has confidence that ethical issues will be brought forward and addressed. Also, in a highly consistent team, people feel valued regardless of their background, age, race, or gender. When problems in the team arise, people accept responsibility rather than look for someone to blame.

Relationships

Effective teams have team members who are quick to praise and slow to criticize each other. Every team member ought to feel appreciated when they make an extra effort to do an excellent job. In teams with positive relationships, conflicts are resolved quickly, and everyone is willing to work collaboratively. Also, team members support each other in improving their skills to perform their job.

TEAM PROFILES

It is beneficial for a team to periodically check the level of trust in the team. Sometimes there are big surprises for some team members and team leaders, and at other times, a good assessment will isolate problems that, once addressed, can be resolved. Looking over hundreds of team assessments, I identified a variety of team profiles.

The Poor Execution and Expertise Team

In this team, trust is low because of lackluster execution and expertise. Often the team is held back because of poor systems and ineffective processes. Too often some leaders blame execution problems only on employee motivation. While that can be a part of the problem, inefficient systems and poor processes can significantly influence the ability to execute.

Communication problems can also be a significant part of the difficulty. This is an easy skill to improve, but leaders often mistakenly assume communication is all that ought to be necessary for team members to understand important information. Add to that a confusing strategy that is not really understood by team members, and the quandary is compounded. Another problem can be poor performance management, where team members who are not contributing are allowed to continue with below-acceptable performance without consequences.

The Nothing Is Ever Good Enough Team

In this team there is a great deal of criticism and little or no praise. Team members are on the lookout for problems and anything done wrong. There is very little recognition and few rewards. Performance reviews focus only on what people need to improve. Team members have few opportunities to learn new skills and progress in their careers.

The Blame-Game Team

In this team, there is a constant effort to blame others for mistakes or problems. Often, in these kinds of teams, people have a few scapegoats who receive most of the blame. This is such a negative existence, the scapegoats often quit as soon as possible. In this team most people resist taking responsibility for problems or difficulties.

The Micromanaged Team

A clear sign of low trust comes from a team where every action or decision is scrutinized and critically evaluated by the team leader or other team members. When people learn new skills, often they will make mistakes, but when a mistake feels like a career-ending event, trust is significantly diminished. In the micromanaged team, people learn quickly that they should only do work that is requested, complete it in an approved way, and never innovate or take initiative to do something new. Trust is diminished because ideas and new approaches from team members are never accepted or welcomed.

CHANGING TRUST IN A TEAM

When assessing trust for a team, we have every team member complete an assessment focused on the team's behavior. When applicable, other stakeholders who interact regularly with the team fill out assessments too. Once all team members have completed the assessment, the results are compiled into a report and provided back to the team for analysis. My analysis of trust data from teams revealed a tighter distribution than was present in the individual trust results. Because of the tighter distribution, I set the low bars at the 25th percentile and the high bars at the 75th percentile. As Figure 12.1 shows, when any of the three elements were below the 25th percentile, trust was diminished significantly. When any element was at the 75th percentile or higher, trust was increased. When all three elements were above the 75th percentile, team trust was at the 88th percentile. Notice that when any of the three elements are below the 25th percentile, trust is negatively impacted.

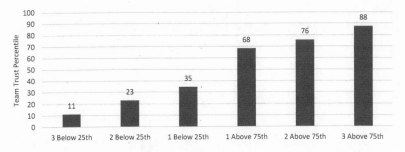

Figure 12.1: Impact of the trifecta elements on team trust.

The implications of this research show that all three elements are necessary for trust to be strong, but it also shows that if just one element is at or above the 75th percentile, trust moves to the 68th percentile, and with two at the 75th percentile, trust then moves to the 76th percentile. When working with teams, I encourage them to identify one element that, if improved, would have the most impact on increasing trust and improving the performance of the team. Any element below the 25th percentile needs some immediate attention. If all the elements are below the 75th percentile, then select the one element that would have the greatest benefit for achieving team goals and objectives. When I examined team trust data to understand which of the three elements has the greatest impact on trust, I found that while all three are high, consistency has the greatest impact, followed by relationships, and with expertise/execution coming last.

TEAM ACTION OR INDIVIDUAL ACTIONS

When teams review their feedback, often they are quick to identify an element that needs improvement, and they generate a team action plan for improvement. For example, a team might want to improve relationships by giving more recognition. In their team action plan, they may have an action such as nominating a team member every month for a recognition award. While that one action might be helpful, to make the most significant changes in the team, I often recommend that each team member also create their own individual action plan. Individual action plans might include things like "Every Friday, I am going to identify one person on the team and write a thank-you note to that person." Having both a team action and individual actions significantly increases the probability of improvement.

Engagement indicates the level of a team's satisfaction, a willingness to recommend the team to others, desire to give extra effort, and confidence that the team will achieve its goals and objectives. It is an excellent indicator of the health of the team and the members' overall satisfaction.

Figure 12.2 shows the results from 1,002 team members from 212 teams. As you can see, team members with low trust scores (i.e., in the bottom 10 percent) had engagement levels at the 27th percentile, on average, but team members with high trust (i.e., in the top 10 percent) had engagement at the 67th percentile.

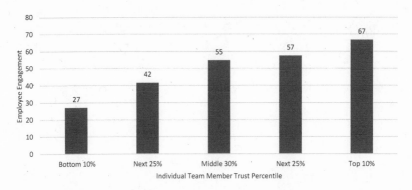

Figure 12.2: Impact of trust on engagement of team members.

The research on engagement highlights how trust in a team impacts each team member's feelings about work, their job, and their ability to achieve goals and objectives. When a person works with others where there is trust, they can relax and concentrate on their job. When trust is low, everyone is on edge. Then, they become unsure about their future, and they are significantly more likely to think about quitting their job.

Trust has a substantial impact on many other issues. Improving trust in a team can significantly improve not only the engagement of team members and their willingness to stay on the team but also the team's ability to achieve goals, find new solutions to problems, and make a real difference in the broader organization. Have you ever worked in a team where you loved coming to work, where you felt lucky to be part of that group, and where you were willing to invest extra time and effort to achieve goals and objectives? Ensuring that trust is high is a key element in creating that kind of a team.

CHAPTER 13

Trust and Confidence

Adam Neumann, the founder of WeWork, believed in creating corporate work environments that could help individuals reach their full potential. His unusual amount of confidence fueled his dream of a utopian society of diverse industries inspiring and motivating each other. In 2019, WeWork was valued as high as $47 billion, but two years later, it was only worth $9 billion. The IPO was canceled in 2019, when investors were highly concerned about the company's substantial financial losses and the arrogant and power-hungry behavior of Neumann, now the former CEO. Yes, Neumann's high confidence convinced people to invest in WeWork. But when his confidence grew to arrogance, it caused people to lose trust in him and his business. He isn't the only one who has experienced a loss of trust when growing self-confidence takes over.

To help people understand their level of confidence, I created a self-assessment. The self-assessment confidence rating has a range in its score from −10 to 10. Using the self-assessment results, we divided people into a low-confidence group (who scored –10 to 0), medium confidence (1 to 5), and high confidence (6 to 10). Figure 13.1 shows the impact of confidence on trust scores by all raters.

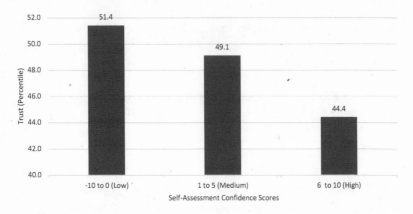

Figure 13.1: Impact of increased confidence on trust.

The graph clearly shows a trend that trust decreases with increased confidence. This was confusing to me; I have always assumed that there is an optimum level of confidence that individuals should seek if they want to maintain trust. I have had good experiences with highly confident individuals I trusted, while on the other hand, I have been deceived by some cunning individuals who used their confidence to manipulate and control. Those with high confidence that I trusted were very optimistic about the future, but at the same time, they always delivered on their commitments. To understand the data better, I took a closer look at those people with high confidence. While the overall average did decline, I found that for 336 leaders with high confidence, their trust scores increased with greater confidence, but for 362 leaders, their trust scores declined despite higher levels of confidence.

Figure 13.2 shows the results for trust along with the three trifecta factors: expertise, consistency, and relationships. All of the differences among the three factors are statistically significant. High confidence clearly helped some people improve their trust and all of the trifecta elements. Additional analysis on the other 16 competencies we measured showed a significant improvement.

Figure 13.2: Differences in outcomes for individuals confidence helped and hurt.

Diving into the data to understand why confidence helps some and hurts others, I discovered that those it hurt scored significantly more negatively on every leadership competency and behavior we measured. These were people who had lots of confidence but low competence.

Can too much confidence hurt people? In 90 percent of the cases, confidence seems to enable people to improve, and the higher the confidence, the higher the effectiveness. But in 10 percent of the cases, when confidence preceded competence, it did have a damaging impact.

What can help people who are overconfident? Balancing your confidence can often feel like walking a never-ending tightrope. You're a jerk if you have too much confidence and a wimp if you have too little. But there is a practice that is closely linked to staying balanced on this path; it's your openness to receiving feedback. You need to be aware of how you are perceived by others. Sometimes you can ask directly, but other times individuals may receive a more accurate evaluation through a 360-degree assessment. Having multiple perspectives from many people will help you know how to improve.

Confidence can magnify trust, but only when a person's confidence matches up with their competence. Assuming you are much more effective than you really are causes others to lose trust in you. If you lie to yourself, you may also lie to others, and when they doubt your consistency and judgment, your relationships suffer.

CHAPTER 14

Trust and Feedback

Being open and acting on the feedback you receive from others is one side of the coin. The other side that heavily influences trust is the type of feedback you give daily to others.

I wondered whether a person who provided positive feedback to others would be more trusted or whether negative or corrective feedback would cause a person to be less trusted. Managers and leaders have some very strong opinions about feedback. I asked 12,555 leaders to select the alternative that would most help employees improve performance:

- Being given specific, constructive suggestions about how to improve

- Being given regular recognition and praise

Eighty-two percent of the leaders selected the first option. The vast majority of people believe that negative or corrective feedback is helpful. Additionally, I questioned that same group of leaders with this statement: "Negative (redirecting) feedback, if delivered appropriately, is effective at improving performance." And 93 percent agreed. Most of them feel that negative feedback can be helpful for a person to improve their performance. Most managers feel it is an important part of their job to provide others with feedback, and that feedback is often negative or redirecting.

In our self-assessment, I asked each individual to indicate their preference for giving others positive or negative (corrective) feedback. Each individual was given 10 paired comparison items to indicate if they preferred or avoided giving positive or negative feedback. I merged the self-assessment data with data from 360-degree assessments. Keep in mind that these raters who completed the assessments were working together regularly in the same organization and knew each other well.

Figure 14.1 shows the results for those who either avoided (516 respondents) or preferred (759 respondents) giving others positive feedback. Here are important things to note from this study: 40 percent of the respondents avoided giving positive feedback. Many people have an assumption that if they give others positive feedback, then they will not listen to or accept the negative feedback when given. Yet those who preferred to give positive feedback were significantly more trusted. They were also rated better for relationships and consistency.

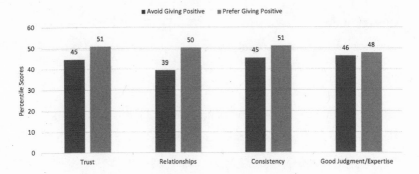

Figure 14.1: Differences in outcomes for individuals
avoiding and giving positive feedback.

In the next case (Figure 14.2), we had 337 respondents who avoided giving negative feedback and 929 who preferred giving negative feedback. Once again, note that 63 percent preferred giving negative feedback, even though many of them reported that delivering negative feedback was a stressful experience. So, what is the impact of a preference for giving others negative feedback? Trust, expertise, consistency, and relationships are all rated significantly lower.

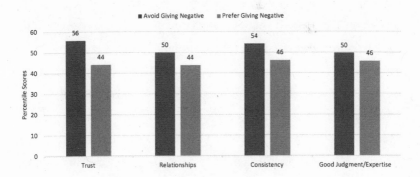

Figure 14.2: Differences in outcomes for individuals
avoiding and giving negative feedback.

THE MAGIC RATIO

John Gottman is a marriage researcher. He attempted to predict whether married couples would stay married or divorce.[20] His process to evaluate the effectiveness of relationships was to observe couples interacting with each other and count the number of positive or negative feelings or interactions the couple would have with each other. In his research, he found that if a couple had a five-to-one ratio of positive to negative interactions, there was a high probability of them staying together. There is a place for negative or corrective feedback, but giving an abundance of positive feedback followed by an occasional suggestion for improvement creates a very different atmosphere than does giving five negatives to one positive. There is no doubt that this ratio can help more than married couples.

Positive relationships are based on the assumption that the other person "has my back" or will take my side and give me the benefit of the doubt. This basically means that even if another person makes a mistake or might be lying, you give the benefit even though you may have doubts. I evaluate leaders' effectiveness at giving feedback by asking others to assess: Does this person give honest feedback in a helpful way? Consider what is "honest" feedback. If a direct report does 90 percent of their work correctly, then honest feedback would be that 90 percent of the feedback they receive from you is positive and 10 percent might be corrective. Corrective feedback is very helpful, but if I feel my manager is out to get me, wants me to fail, and does not have my best interests at heart, I will not be very receptive to that negative feedback. Trust is built through honesty in all of your communication.

---

20 John Gottman and Julie Schwartz Gottman, *The Science of Couples and Family Therapy: Behind the Scenes at the "Love Lab"* (New York: W. W. Norton, 2018).

People need to hear the great things they are doing just as much as the ways to improve.

A strong preference to give others negative/corrective feedback also damages trust. Developing the habit of looking for opportunities to provide positive feedback creates an environment that builds trust. When trust exists, an occasional corrective suggestion creates a trusting atmosphere where corrective feedback can actually build more trust. Trust is built because others believe "you have their back," and in turn "they have your back."

CHAPTER 15

The Loss of Trust

C had was hired as the vice president of sales for a technology firm. He was very impressive, dressed well, had a charming personality, and was bold and self-assured on sales calls. Under his leadership, sales in the company increased significantly. He was personally responsible for bringing in sales from several major clients. The company owners were extremely pleased that he was part of the firm.

After several months, Chad approached the owners with a great idea. He felt that if he had his name on some of the articles and publications associated with the technology, buyers would consider him more of an expert. The owners agreed, and soon it appeared as though he had been an integral part of the company from the beginning. Eventually, the company garnered the interest of a prestigious university, and Chad was quick to closely manage the relationship. In delivering the technology, he insisted that he would play a leading role, which was unusual for a person in sales. He insisted that the client communicate through him only, and ensured that his name was closely associated with the project.

Chad was always pleased with himself when he was able to make a sale at prices that were significantly higher than standard retail. Chad made several decisions without checking with the company owners, and eventually the owners started to think that they should change the name of the company to Chad, Inc. While he started out being trusted, within a few years, he had lost all trust. He did not want to be a player on the team; he wanted to *be* the team.

The owners decided to fire Chad. Chad was shocked by the news. All he had done was make the company successful. Chad asked if he could continue to be an independent contractor because many clients had close relationships with only him. The owners knew that keeping Chad involved would probably make the company more money, but in the end, they simply did not trust him.

WHAT HAPPENS TO A LEADER WHO IS NOT TRUSTED?

A loss of trust leads to a variety of negative impacts. For example, in our analyses, the leader's overall leadership effectiveness after a loss of trust is rated at the 13th percentile. Employee engagement of their direct reports is at the 30th percentile, and 42 percent of their direct reports are thinking about quitting. Only 7 percent of direct reports are willing to put forth extra effort, and only 5 percent of the untrusted leaders were part of the high-potential pool. When trust is lost, effectiveness is gone, direct reports are disengaged, and many people are looking for a way out.

Many leaders live in fear of saying the wrong thing or doing something that might offend a colleague. While we are all seeking ways to improve social justice and provide more inclusive work environments that promote belonging, progress can at times be a tender process. What leads to rifts in relationships that slowly fester and grow larger? By doing additional analysis on the data set, I was able to identify the main factors that lead to a loss of trust. The factors are listed in order of their impact.

Damaged Relationships

At the top of the list, I found that when relationships are damaged, trust is lost. People do not trust those they dislike.

Several years ago, I coached a division president who had very low scores in trust. When I inquired why his results were so negative, he replied, "I avoid developing positive relationships with my team because I never know when I will have to fire one of them."

The only problem with his approach was that his poor relationship with team members caused most of them to quit before he could fire them. Team members do not need to be a leader's best friend, but they do need to be respected and valued and to feel that their manager has their back.

Saying One Thing, Doing Another

Duplicity will also destroy trust. Many leaders are unaware of their duplicity because of a tendency to tell others what they want to hear instead of providing them with accurate feedback.

In a meeting, Janet asked her manager, "How am I doing in my job so far?"

The manager replied, "Great."

What Janet heard was that there was no problem with her performance. A few weeks later, Janet had a performance review with her manager. In the discussion, her manager mentioned a few areas that concerned her and needed improvement.

The manager's feedback was a big surprise. Last week she was great, but now there were problems? Janet's frustration with the duplicity of her manager continued to grow with the inconsistent messaging she was receiving. Many leaders tend to overpromise and underdeliver, and when that happens, trust is lost. Leaders need to be careful about what they say, because direct reports will remember.

Claiming Expertise without the Knowledge

Sharing your expertise and knowledge can build trust in others. Giving others inaccurate or misleading information will cause them to lose trust quickly. It is impossible for leaders to have all the answers and to be knowledgeable about every issue. Problems arise when leaders give their uninformed opinions as if they are facts. Leaders could easily avoid this problem if they would only gather data from more knowledgeable experts.

Several years ago, I worked with a colleague who was perceived by others as being very smart. Often, he would answer questions by saying, "There are three reasons for that," and he would proceed to give the three reasons. After a while, I noticed that the second and third reasons were often not very compelling, and occasionally, he would never get around to the second and third reason.

That was his magic trick. Most of us, if given enough time, can come up with three reasons for anything but typically not when you begin a conversation. He discovered that if you talk about one reason for a little while, the second reason will often occur to you. After watching him do this multiple times, people would catch on to the magic trick and figure out that he was trying to appear smarter than he really was. His reason for doing this was to improve his credibility, but eventually, people would discover what he was doing, and this only hurt his long-term credibility.

The One-Person Show

People in this category believe that by acting independently, they can make their own decisions, avoid distractions from others, and take full credit for their accomplishments. The problem with people who want to act independently is that organizations work well only when people find ways to cooperate and collaborate. Those who resist cooperation and prefer their independence are not as trusted.

Cheryl was in charge of special projects. Whatever project was assigned to her, she would make all the decisions, even though all of her projects were being utilized by other departments. Cheryl had a lot of experience in the company and thought her experience gave her the right to act independently. She worked very hard and always seemed overwhelmed. When a new project was given to her, there was a brief explanation of the project objectives, and then Cheryl would go to work but never communicate about her plan or progress until she was finished. Once she finished, she handed the project off, and if the next person involved in the project ever asked questions, Cheryl would become very defensive. Because of Cheryl's approach, many of the other departments started to do projects on their own, and Cheryl was eventually let go.

Resisting and Rejecting Feedback

When people first start working, they typically ask for a lot of feedback from others. As they age, the willingness to ask for feedback decreases for many. Those who continue to ask for feedback throughout their career end up being more trusted.

I looked at data from over 62,000 leaders for a study shown in Figure 15.1. Note that the effectiveness at asking for and acting on feedback (the first bar) decreases as leaders age. Older leaders, on average, are less effective than younger leaders at asking for feedback. The second bar shows the asking-for-feedback score for those in the top quartile on trust. Note that those scores do not decrease with age, but rather, there is a small increase. The third bar represents the percentage of people in the top quartile who asks for and acts on feedback. These percentages decrease from 50 percent at ages 25 to 35 to 18 percent at 61 years and older. This study clearly demonstrates that those who continue to ask for feedback as they age are more trusted.

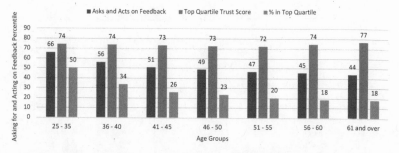

Figure 15.1: Leaders who ask and act on feedback as they age are more trusted.

The Pushy Driver for Results

Those leaders who only push and don't know how to pull end up losing the trust of others. Those who know how to pull will start by creating positive emotional connections with others. Rather than demand that a team member works harder, inspiring leaders find ways to get their people excited about accomplishing a difficult goal.

For the study depicted in Figure 15.2, I examined 360-degree data from 85,904 leaders. I wanted to understand the impact of effectiveness that push (drive for results) and pull (inspiring and motivating others) have on trust. Average scores were those below the 75th percentile, while high scores were those in the top quartile. Note that when both push and pull are average, trust is at the 40th percentile (10 percentile points below average). Moving either push or pull into the top quartile improves trust, but improving both puts trust into the 79th percentile. The point this study makes is that leaders do not need to stop pushing and only pull to build trust. The secret to having the highest levels of trust is to both push and pull.

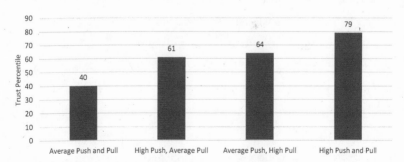

Figure 15.2: The push and pull impact on trust.

TRUST IS DECLINING

The Edelman Trust Barometer indicates that trust is currently at a low level in the United States.[21] The results across the globe are based on a sample of more than 33,000 respondents. The index averages trust in NGOs, businesses, government, and the media. The US results are at the same level as those in Colombia, France, and South Africa.

Social trust is based on the belief that most people will do the right thing most of the time. If I get new medical insurance and go to the hospital, I trust that they will honor the insurance and send the bill to the insurance company, and the insurance company will pay the bill. I trust that if I order food at the fast-food restaurant, I will get the food I ordered and pay the price on the menu, and if there is a mistake, they will make things right. Social trust assumes that most people will make intelligent choices and do the right thing most of the time. It assumes that people will follow the advice of experts. It assumes that people will follow the rules.

Our research on trust clearly shows that economies with lower trust have a lower GDP. But in high-trust societies, good outcomes follow. In high-trust societies, corruption is lower, bribery is rare, and elections are fair—with the losers accepting the results. In high-trust societies, we have the rule of law. We allow differences of opinion.

In low-trust societies, it is harder to get a loan, harder to buy a used car, more difficult to sell a car, and more difficult to get services because we distrust service providers. Low trust slows down the economy, slows down economic progress, breaks up marriages, impacts relationships, and destroys happiness.

---

21 Edelman, *Edelman Trust Barometer 2021*, 2021, www.edelman.com/sites/g/files/aatuss191/files/2021-01/2021-edelman-trust-barometer.pdf.

Trust is the oil that makes an engine run, and when you run out of oil, your engine freezes up. In a study I did with over 99,000 managers with assessments from an average of five direct reports, when a leader has low trust, 48 percent of their employees want to quit, only 17 percent are willing to work harder, and only 19 percent think that the organization will achieve its goals.

The word *attention* is derived from the Latin term *attendere*, which means "to reach toward." If you are willing to reach toward the people around you, give them your time and attention, and earn their trust, you'll experience the astounding benefits of those efforts.

Every individual can have an impact on the social trust in a society. It's difficult to change the world or change your country, but I do believe that you can change yourself. I also believe that your trust impacts the trust of others. Trust is contagious—the more trust you have, the more others will have.

CHAPTER 16

Rebuilding Trust

The process for rebuilding trust may seem redundant. Isn't it the same as building trust? In many ways, these insights will be similar to those discussed in previous chapters. But the context is very different. The individual standing in this place does not have a clean slate nor a fresh start. So, although they must once again establish the same pillars of the trifecta of trust, their journey will be different.

Leaders who have lost trust need to start the restoration process by making a public and sincere acknowledgment of their faults. Letting others know that you feel sorry for past mistakes allows them to reset their expectations. When you are driving down the freeway with other vehicles and you notice a car in front of you shifting into your lane, what you want to see is a turn signal so you know for sure that they are moving into your lane; it also shows that they are aware of you and have considered your concerns as well as their own. Signaling your intention lets others know that you want to make a change. Signaling your intention to increase trust is a critical part of improvement. But it's just the beginning.

In 2020, an unexpected character emerged on the global stage as a source of information and truth-telling that you could trust: Governor Andrew Cuomo of New York. His daily no-nonsense coronavirus briefings were watched and talked about by millions. He was becoming revered for his strong leadership in a crisis and was even mentioned as an unlikely hopeful to upset the 2020 presidential election. As quick as his rise to fame was his public downfall. Revelations about a serious character flaw began to emerge: his inappropriate attentions toward women.

While Cuomo isn't one to quickly apologize, he eventually issued a statement: "I never intended to offend anyone or cause any harm. I never intended to make anyone feel uncomfortable, but these are allegations that New Yorkers deserve answers to."

While the allegations continued to mount against him in the coming months, on August 10, 2021, after a decade of serving as governor, he resigned.[22]

There are some actions that make rebuilding trust almost impossible. The sheer number of accusations against Governor Cuomo was an uphill battle he could not win while serving in office. He learned that the world is no longer tolerant of certain behaviors. He said that he now sees "the world through the eyes of my daughters" and realizes why his throwback behavior made women uncomfortable in the #MeToo era.

We will all make mistakes. We say things and do things we are not proud of, and the former governor will hopefully forever think twice about how his actions and attentions are perceived. Not surprisingly, he expressed no interest in running for office again. His path to

---

22 Marlene Lenthang, "NY Gov. Andrew Cuomo Gives Farewell Address: A Timeline of the Sexual Harassment Allegations," ABC News, August 23, 2021.

rebuilding trust with those around him will be long. No amount of prestige or power can save you from a significant loss of trust, but in some circumstances, with some people, trust can be rebuilt.

THERE IS HOPE

For most individuals who find themselves wondering if they can possibly repair what was broken, the answer is yes. You need to repair it. Perhaps the worst part of our broad "cancel" culture is not giving individuals the opportunity to make amends. There are times when there is an absolute need for an individual to step away from a position. But before joining the masses of stone throwers on Twitter, perhaps we can remember that we are all humans, we all make mistakes, and we should allow people the opportunity to make amends. Remember, you may offend someone, you may completely blow your budget, or you may give someone really bad advice, and maybe you'll pull a Larry David by losing it, quitting your job, and then showing up the next week pretending it didn't happen (yes, that actually happened when he was at SNL). Once trust is lost, it can be rebuilt. Of course, some people will argue that it can't and it's better to move on, but I have evidence it is possible.

There has been a lot of wisdom about repairing trust in close relationships between partners or family members. However, the relationships between colleagues at work can be different, and I wanted to understand how trust is rebuilt in that setting. That rebuilding process with coworkers is just as important to focus on as the trust you build with customers.

Rather than rely on conventional wisdom, I identified data from

564 leaders who participated in a 360-degree assessment that measured their skill at generating trust and 48 other important leadership
behaviors. The leaders in this study were all assessed as having trust
scores that were considered a fatal flaw (i.e., their results were at or
below the 10th percentile). Each of these leaders was given feedback
and created an improvement plan. After 18 to 24 months, each participant was reassessed on the same set of behaviors.

Examining the posttest results (Figure 16.1), I found that 87 percent, or 493 people, made a small incremental improvement. Their
trust score went from the 6th to the 16th percentile. Trust continues to be a negative issue for these individuals. However, 13 percent
of the people in this study (71 individuals) were able to move from
the 6th percentile to the 66th percentile on average. That is a huge
shift, going from untrusted to above average on trust. This is a highly
significant shift, and I would conclude that this group was able to
restore trust.

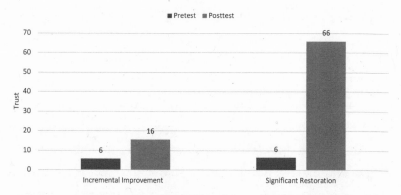

Figure 16.1: Difference between incremental improvement and restoration.

TWELVE ACTIONS FOR REBUILDING TRUST

It is possible to restore trust, but it is difficult. After all, only 13 percent of the people in this study made a significant change. So the question I had after looking at this data was "What did the significant restoration group do that made a big difference?" After analyzing the data, I identified 12 specific actions that enabled the significant shift for these leaders who intended to successfully rebuild trust.

Balance Individual Needs with Results

Plastered on the walls of numerous organizations is the phrase "People are our greatest asset." The phrase seems especially hypocritical whenever an organization has layoffs. Employees may sometimes wonder, "What is more important—my results or me?" The stark and unpleasant reality for the vast majority of employees is, if they do not deliver the expected results, they may be fired from their job. Most people do not want to be absolved of all their responsibilities at work, but they occasionally have issues that require consideration and flexibility.

As I know from not just my life experience but extensive research on trust, having a personal relationship is vitally important in building and repairing trust. We are more likely to trust people when we have a positive personal relationship with them. Note that the issue here is the balance of individual needs and work, not that only individuals are important and results are not important. Those leaders who need to build trust must spend time and effort building new relationships and reinforcing existing relationships. If relationship building feels like hard or difficult work, people will do it only when required. The solution for many people is to find a style and approach to building relationships that are comfortable and reinforcing.

I enjoy some relationship building, but I sometimes dislike meet-and-greet cocktail events with clients when traveling. Typically, I know very few people at these events, and making small talk with strangers can be draining. During one cocktail hour that I was not looking forward to, I asked myself, *What do I enjoy doing when meeting people I do not know?* I immediately thought, *I enjoy interviewing people about their work experience or their approach to leading others.* When I went to the event, I spent all of my time gathering data, which provided new insights and made me happy, and all of those I talked to seemed to enjoy talking about themselves and their work.

Relationship building is like any skill. For example, consider learning to play golf or tennis. If you are a poor golfer, chances are you are not going to enjoy golfing. But if you improve, you will no doubt enjoy golf more. By practicing relationship building, you can enhance your capability, and you will find your enjoyment also increases.

Be a Role Model

Some people want to be rebels. They want to chart their own course, find their own way, and do their own thing. Others tend to distrust rebels. It is always interesting to watch young children act like their parents. Modeling behavior has a dramatic impact on the way others behave.

While giving a tour to a group of other executives, the former CEO of Disney, Michael Eisner, saw some garbage on the sidewalk and casually bent down to pick it up and throw it away. He understood the vision of Disneyland and the importance of keeping the park clean. A few employees saw him do that, and the next day, thousands of employees had heard that even the CEO of Disney picks up garbage, making it just as important for everyone in the organization.

No doubt, you might be unaware of actions people notice when you are not being a role model. Often these might be little things to you but important to others. It helps to have a trusted confidant to keep you apprised about your actions and unintended consequences. Make a list of things you ask others to do that you don't always do yourself.

Often, people with extremely low trust scores have done something to someone where an apology is necessary. A key part of the apology is acknowledging what you did wrong. An apology needs to be authentic, but that is hard to do if you feel angry, frustrated, or belittled. When you apologize, you need to acknowledge your behavior and take responsibility. Victims will be very reluctant to start increasing their trust without an apology and an acknowledgment of what you did wrong. Many individuals struggle to know the right words to say to convey a sincere message and desire to change. It doesn't hurt to practice the apology with a trusted friend who could help give you feedback and direction for that critical conversation. Because this is a challenging process, doing it will be helpful to you in changing your behavior in the future.

Ensure Good Judgment in Decisions

Decisions in an organization are like a target that is painted on the decision maker's back. When you decide alone, with no input or involvement from others, you are the only one with that target. Research has shown that most of the time, involving others will improve the effectiveness of a decision. You can decide who to involve and who not to involve. You can share the issues with others, gather their insight, and make the decision alone, or you can gather a group together and insist that you decide based on the group's consensus. Depending on the time available, the nature of what you are deciding, and the insights or biases, you decide the level of involvement that is most appropriate.

Improving your judgment may involve additional study, reading, and learning on your part. Many people think about going to school as a learning event and then working as an opportunity to apply the knowledge they learned in school. The problem is that most of what we learned in school is out of date and replaced by new methods or discoveries. Find a way to keep current and up to date.

Encourage Cooperation

Many people like to work independently and do their own thing. There are various motives for working this way that range from being an introvert to being extremely competitive. Assessing more than 100,000 leaders on their effectiveness at collaboration, I found that out of 16 competencies, collaboration comes in 14th. In other words, leaders are not great at the behavior; it ranks third from the last! I also asked managers to rate how important collaboration was for a leader to be successful. Leaders ranked collaboration as the third most important behavior to possess.

I have found in the majority of our clients a strong desire to improve collaboration in their organization. One executive commented, "We acquired this portfolio of companies because they would be worth more together than they were working independently. But the only way they can increase their value is by working together and collaborating. Without collaboration we get no synergy." Because being more collaborative improves your relationships with others, this will have a positive impact on trust. Leaders know it is important, but they just have to do it more.

Resolve Conflicts

Often when trust is low, conflict is a significant part of the problem. Conflict is not going to disappear unless there is some motivation and willingness to change. Most conflicts will only be resolved when at least one person reaches out in humility with a strong desire to resolve the conflict.

Unfortunately, some people don't want to resolve the conflict; they want to be declared the winner. With that approach, the conflict will never be resolved. Research shows that the greater the conflict in a work group, the lower the engagement, the higher the turnover, and the lower the productivity.

In a study summarized in Figure 16.2, I examined data from 90,338 leaders who were assessed on their ability to resolve conflict. Each leader was assessed by 13 evaluators, including their manager, peers, direct reports, and others. I then looked at the direct reports' willingness to go the extra mile. Note that as a leader's ability to resolve conflict increases, so does the percentage of direct reports willing to give extra effort. The effect of this is a dramatic increase in productivity.

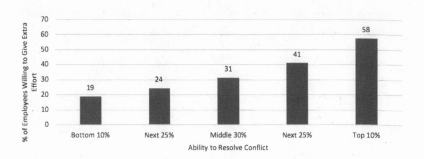

Figure 16.2: Impact of resolving conflict.

The common assumption about conflict is that those who are having the conflict will, in time, resolve the conflict. However, be aware that conflict in a work group may be hurting your performance and ultimately negatively impact your career. Regardless of your position, who's right and who's wrong, it would be best if you committed to helping resolve the conflict. Conflicts can be caused by poor performance, inaccurate expectations, poor communication, personal traits, incompatible values, or lack of resources. Whatever the cause, be determined to resolve the conflict.

There are four basic steps in resolving conflict. Start with *communication*. Get everyone involved talking. A huge part of communication is listening. Ensure that each person is correctly hearing what the other person is saying. Next, focus on the *implications* of the conflict. Describe the negative effects it has. Have each person describe how the conflict negatively impacts getting the job done and how it affects their stress, feelings about work, and satisfaction. Then offer *solutions*. Ask each person for potential solutions to resolve the conflict. Brainstorm additional ideas; often, having at least three ideas will yield a better solution. Finally, make a *commitment*. Have each person make a personal commitment for resolving the conflict, and set a deadline for change.

Communicate, Communicate, Communicate

Several years ago, I had an interview with a woman in her office. I knocked on the door and sat down to start the discussion.

Before I could start, the woman said, "I was moving some boxes this morning that stained my dress. I just wanted you to know that it was an accident so you would not think that I am an unkempt slob!" She was sitting behind her desk, and I could not see the stain, but she felt compelled to mention the stain anyway. Have you had a clothing mishap and had the same thought: "Everyone will notice"? You'll usually find that few people actually notice.

In a similar way, have you ever assumed that other people were astutely aware of problems you were having on a project but then found out that no one had a clue? You dropped hints, rolled your eyes, and even made groans of frustration, and from your perspective, everyone should have noticed you were having problems. We believe others are more aware and informed than they really are. We think that because we tell other people about a significant event one week ahead of time, they will remember. In reality, to communicate well, we need to overcommunicate.

Poor communication can be a significant cause of loss of trust. Letting others have advance notice of the where, why, how, and what is happening is a critically important skill. In my research on communication, I have found that this is one of the easiest skills to improve. Can a person overcommunicate? We all know this is possible, but most people's persistent problem is that they communicate too little. When others don't know about something that is important or are confused regarding what to do or where to go, that can quickly lead to distrust. A beneficial first step to restoring trust is to increase the amount and quality of communication with others significantly.

Give Honest Feedback

I looked at a data set of over 100,000 leaders who were assessed on how effective they were at giving honest feedback to others in a helpful way. The first question I had was "Would leaders who delivered honest feedback be more trusted?" The results shown in Figure 16.3 conclusively demonstrate that trust increased as leaders improved in their ability to deliver honest feedback.

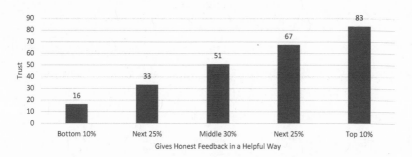

Figure 16.3: Leaders giving honest feedback are more trusted.

The second question was "What is honest feedback?" In an informal poll of my colleagues, when I asked them, "What does it mean to give honest feedback to others?" they used words like "giving tough feedback" and "telling people what you really think rather than just being nice." One person said, "To be honest, it has to be difficult to deliver and something that needs to be fixed." In other words, people believe that honest feedback tends to be more negative than positive.

I created a self-assessment that measures a leader's preference for giving negative and positive feedback. Leaders can express a preference to either give or avoid giving positive or negative feedback. I gathered data on more than 10,000 leaders using this assessment and have been able to match up the self-assessment with 360-degree evaluations from others where we measured trust. I was able to match up the results for 588 leaders.

I divided leaders into those who tended to prefer or avoid giving positive or negative feedback. I then examined the level of trust that people had in these leaders. The results were statistically significant, indicating that those who preferred giving negative feedback were less trusted. As presented in Figure 16.4, those who preferred giving negative feedback were rated in the 41st percentile on trust, while those who avoided giving negative feedback were rated in the 53rd percentile. Those who preferred to give positive feedback also showed a statistically significant higher score on trust, being rated at the 48th percentile, compared to those who avoided giving positive feedback, being rated at the 41st percentile.

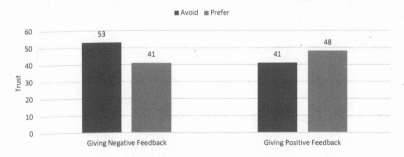

Figure 16.4: Impact on trust of giving negative or positive feedback.

This research has caused me to question the assumption that giving honest feedback implies giving mostly negative or corrective feedback. Nearly all—99 percent—of the actions of the people we work with each day are the right or correct actions, and only occasionally do they do something wrong. If we notice and talk about only the things a person does wrong, are we being honest?

Let's assume that another person does 50 percent of their work wrong. If we only talk to that person about what they do wrong, is that completely accurate? The more I look at this data, the more apparent it is that honest feedback is mostly positive feedback with an occasional suggestion for change or improvement. Having a strong preference for giving people corrective feedback and avoiding positive feedback doesn't give people a fully accurate depiction of their performance, and it certainly does not build trust. Trust from others comes from having them believe you have their back and their best interest at heart.

John Gottman's research on the magic ratio (five positives to one negative interaction) and my own research on preference for giving positive versus negative feedback reinforce the point that trust is built by letting others know that you are on their side. Your goal in giving honest feedback should be to recognize others when they do good work and, when they occasionally make a mistake, to help them understand what they did wrong and how they can correct the error.

Work on Yourself

One of the biggest problems with rebuilding trust is that people often don't exactly know what they need to do. When they realize that they are not trusted, they form some theories about what caused the lack of trust and what they need to do to improve. Rather than confirm their assumptions by communicating with others, they move ahead and take action. Often, their theories are wrong, and the trust is not restored. It takes a great deal of humility to ask others for feedback. Usually, upon receiving feedback, people debate and rationalize their actions rather than accept it. Even worse, some people ask for feedback but then do nothing to change.

In the study depicted in Figure 16.5, I looked at data from more than 85,000 leaders. They were rated on their level of trust and the extent to which they looked for opportunities to get feedback on themselves and made a real effort to improve based on the feedback.

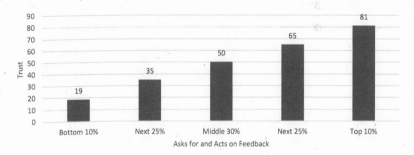

Figure 16.5: Those who ask for and act on feedback from others are more trusted.

As you can see from the graph, there is a direct relationship between a person's willingness and ability to ask for and act on feedback and the extent to which others trust them. Consider situations where you inadvertently offended someone. The only way you find out about doing this is through feedback from others. Most people have read the Hans Christian Andersen story "The Emperor's New Clothes," where the tailors create a new suit invisible to those who are unfit or stupid. The emperor parades the streets utterly naked while all his subjects admire his "clothes" because no one except a small child is brave enough to tell the emperor he is walking around naked. In much the same way, many people assume they are trusted when they are not, because they resist asking for feedback.

Too often, when people do ask for feedback, they are only told what other people feel they want to hear. For example, a senior leader might say, "How was that meeting?" only to hear "Terrific" or "Fantastic" from their direct reports. A much better way to ask for feedback is to say, "What could I have done in the meeting to make it more effective?" What you might hear from a question like this is "It would be helpful if we had come to a definite conclusion about the way forward" or "A few people's comments took up all the time, and others who were more knowledgeable never commented." Asking for more specific feedback indicates that you are open and willing to hear critical critiques, and it makes it easier for others to provide actionable feedback.

Be a Coach and Mentor to Others

Think about a coach or mentor you've had in your life. How do you perceive those who have spent time and energy helping you develop? Typically, we think of these people with fondness and appreciation. Looking at employee survey data for groups who were dissatisfied, I found that one of the largest single complaints voiced by employees is the lack of development opportunities. People naturally want to grow, learn, and develop new skills.

For many people in their final years in a job, one of the things they are most proud of is that they have taken many people under their wing and helped them in their development journey. Being a coach and mentor to others also impacts the extent to which you are trusted. To study this, I looked at assessments from more than 90,000 direct reports who rated their managers on their effectiveness at being a coach or mentor, along with the extent to which these managers were trusted. As can be seen in Figure 16.6, the most influential coaches and mentors were also the most trusted.

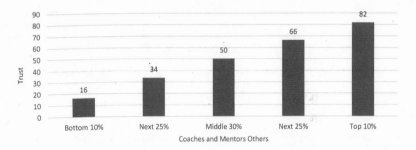

Figure 16.6: Those who are skilled at coaching and mentoring others are more trusted.

You do not need to be a manager to be a coach and mentor. I've found that many of the best coaches are individual contributors that take pride in their ability to help their colleagues learn and develop. Too often, individual contributors feel that being the only person who understands a specific process or function provides them with job security and increases their value to the organization. In other words, they attempt to hold the organization hostage.

What organizations value are people who can support others in learning and developing new skills and knowledge. What's better than one intelligent engineer? Two intelligent engineers. The value of the person who coaches and mentors others is significantly higher, because they are a person who is trusted.

Keep Focused on the Big Picture

Often, the visual used to demonstrate a lack of wider focus is an ostrich with its head buried in the sand. Sometimes people get so caught up in their job or function that they refuse to look at how their job or role affects the larger goals and strategies of the organization.

What's interesting about ostriches is that they bury their heads in the sand because they have eggs buried in the sand and are simply turning the eggs to ensure that they are warm on all sides. Their purpose is not to hide from predators but, rather, to fulfill a more prominent strategic purpose: to take care of their future chicks.

It is very easy for anyone to get so caught up in their particular job or function that they lose sight of what else is happening around them. For example, when people run or ride their bikes, they often assume they are working hard and moving fast, but when another runner or biker passes them, they suddenly get a reality check. Having one focus on their internal job or function can cause people to lack perspective, and often this inward focus causes others to lose trust.

To demonstrate the importance of a big-picture focus, we looked at results for more than 90,000 leaders who were evaluated by their direct reports. Direct reports rated their managers on their clear perspective between the overall picture and the details and how much they trusted the managers' ideas and opinions. As Figure 16.7 vividly demonstrates, those leaders who were able to maintain a clear perspective between details and the big picture had significantly higher levels of trust.

In today's busy environment, it's so easy to get engrossed in the tiny details, emails, voice mails, meetings, and deadlines that we forget to look outside our immediate task to ensure we are doing the right thing and will have the most significant impact. This is a constant battle, and I'm fairly certain that it will only get more difficult in the future.

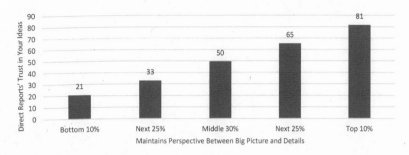

Figure 16.7: Leaders' ideas are more trusted when they maintain perspective.

Inspire and Motivate

Most people learn early in life about the importance of achieving results and being accountable. I have discussed the aspects of push and pull throughout this book. A leader striving to rebuild trust might be hesitant to "push" any direct reports. But as I described earlier, the research shows that leaders who both push and pull have greater trust.

Looking at Zenger Folkman's global data on more than 100,000 leaders, I found that driving for results was the fourth most positive-rated competency, but inspiring others was rated as the least effective competency. When I asked direct reports which competency was most important, inspiring others was rated as number one.

I have discovered that most people are fairly good at pushing but are not as clear about how to pull. It's also clear that being effective at inspiring can have an even more positive impact on the younger generation of leaders. For Figure 16.8, I examined data on more than 5,000 employees who had rated their leaders as being high in both push and pull. Note how the trust levels tend to be highest with younger participants in the assessment.

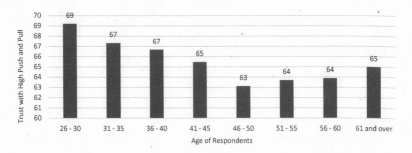

Figure 16.8: High push and pull has greater impact on younger employees.

Many people are confused about what they can do to be more inspiring. After researching data from thousands of leaders, my colleague Jack Zenger and I discovered that most suggestions for how to renew trust will also make a person more inspiring. The specific suggestions connected to our research are the same actions recommended in the rest of this chapter: Rather than pushing others to accomplish objectives, inspiring leaders get others excited about accomplishing objectives by making a positive emotional connection, being a role model, cooperating, communicating, helping others develop new skills, and keeping people focused on the vision and direction of the organization.

Be Open to New Ideas

It is often easy to point out why a new idea will not work, but people who have a terrible habit of doing that are less trusted. Finding ways to improve ideas rather than discouraging them builds the trust of others. Not every new idea is a good idea, but everyone wants to be heard and respected.

You have probably been in a situation where a bad idea in a brainstorming session led to an excellent idea. At its heart, this action is basically about being optimistic. One way to increase optimism is to be more motivated for the success of others. Unfortunately, some people are only motivated for their own success, often at the expense of others. That is a sure formula to reduce trust.

Being motivated for the success of others begins by showing concern for others and being aware of their well-being and problems. For many people, failures cause them to be pessimistic, but learning from failures helps you identify valuable information that can facilitate future success. Another factor that creates pessimism is conflict. Working hard to reduce conflict and increase cooperation will create favorable environments that foster trust.

TRUST CAN BE RESTORED

It is not easy, but making progress on some of the most critical factors linked to rebuilding trust will allow you and your organization to repair damage caused by the loss of trust. You should start the process by reviewing the factors and identifying significant problems, neutral factors, and existing strengths. Once you have done this exercise, review your analysis with a trusted colleague to ensure they agree.

The next step is to communicate to others your intention to change. Often, this needs to be accompanied by apologies to those who have been negatively impacted. When you are ready, start by creating a plan for change with follow-up dates and a person who will hold you accountable. It will take time and repeated efforts to rebuild trust. Be aware that mistakes on your part put you in an even worse position to restore trust, so be consistent in your efforts. What should help you stay on track is how much the trust of others renews and invigorates you. The trust of others will increase your happiness and engagement. It will increase your desire to help others and make a difference in the world.

There is excellent data to suggest that if trust can be increased in a country, the citizens' economic prosperity will increase along with personal happiness and safety. If you can increase the level of trust in an organization, that organization will be more successful, it will more easily accomplish important goals, and its employees will be more engaged and committed.

The formula for increasing trust is simple.

First, improve relationships. The quickest and easiest way to improve relationships is to pay attention to them. A person earns a good relationship. Those who put in effort and pay their dues receive the reward of having a positive relationship. Those who are distracted or pay attention to other things will have worse relationships. With relationships, in the long run you get what you deserve.

Second, share your expertise, and when you lack expertise, get smart. Every person is responsible for understanding their job and learning how to improve their performance. Over time, people get lazy. When people stay in the same job for a long time, many start to assume that they know all they need to know, and so they start to coast on the job. When this happens, the trust that others have in them diminishes.

Third, be consistent. Stop writing checks you can't cash. Before you say, "I will do that by Friday!" make sure you have the time and are willing to make the effort to deliver on your commitments. When you tell others you will do something, they always remember your commitments, but you often forget, so keep track of your commitments. When you fail to deliver, humbly ask for forgiveness.

If you do these three things well, you will be trusted. And if you are trusted, life will be better. If you can increase the trust others have in you, your personal prosperity will increase, you will be happier, and your satisfaction with life will increase.

The Beatles once sang, "All you need is love," but love is an outcome, and after spending two years researching and analyzing every aspect of trust, I would adjust those lyrics to declare, "All you need is trust!"

Afterword

I t may be due to the nature of my work, but I have a difficult time trusting the advice of just one person. I have seen the power of gaining multiple perspectives from different cultures, age groups, and levels of experience through my lifetime of building and administering 360-degree assessments. I view the feedback I gather from these remarkable leaders as an astonishing gift that I'm able to sift through, find patterns in, answer questions about, and learn from every day. I guess I really do love my golden database. My desire is that the experiences and statistics gathered from these leaders have given you some insights, a clear pathway, and a hope that will empower you to build or repair trust in your life.

I said at the start that this book would be based not on observational theories but on research. Now that I have shared the bulk of the research, allow me to close this section with a few observations from my life. I grew up with parents who taught me a lot about trust, hard work, and integrity. Over the past 40 years, building two different companies, I have frequently observed and experienced the failings of men and women. I've seen individuals abuse company funds. I've worked with people who took advantage of others by shifting their responsibilities while contributing little to the organization. I've spent time developing a future leader who then tried to destroy my work. I've been in courtrooms. I have felt despair after realizing that I had broken someone's trust. I've also experienced the enduring walk of gaining it back. I've learned there are some relationships you should fight to repair and others where it's best to part and move on. Either pathway is not easy.

We can sometimes think of experiences in our lives where we have inspired someone or did a great job at driving for results, but our experiences with trust tend to run much deeper. The lessons from trust leave an imprint that can uplift but sometimes break you. You don't have to stay broken. You can learn to forgive and trust others and yourself. You can take the time and energy to earn and increase the trust of those around you. You can build a high-trust organization that experiences the incredible benefits of less burnout, more energy, more closeness with colleagues, and higher productivity. Every individual deserves a boss they can trust.

Trust is a behavior that seems elusive at times and hard for individuals to understand, and yet, as I have demonstrated, its enormous influence can be accurately measured. Trust can predict the wealth or poverty of a nation, and it can also predict the success or failure of an individual. You can feel trust when people commit to do a difficult task or follow you through uncharted waters. You feel trust when someone you care about is accused of doing something wrong and you say, "I know they would never do that!" Trust bubbles up when the results are not what you expected, but you have confidence that those around you can help turn things around. Trust can be felt, trust can be measured, trust can be built, and trust can be repaired. To truly understand trust in its most simplistic form, it comes down to expertise, consistency, and positive relationships: the trifecta of trust.

Index

About the Author

Joe Folkman is globally recognized as a top leader in the field of psychometrics and leadership. He is the cofounder and president of Zenger Folkman, a firm specializing in 360-degree assessments, leadership, and organizational development. He has over 30 years of experience consulting with some of the world's most prestigious and successful organizations, public and private. As the 2021 recipient of ATD's Distinguished Contribution to Talent Development Award, Joe was recognized for his extensive research and contributions to the learning and development industry.

He has frequently contributed to *Harvard Business Review*, *Forbes*, *Business Insider*, *CLO Magazine*, and *Talent Quarterly*. His research has also been repeatedly featured in venues such as *Business Week*, *Fortune*, the *New York Times*, the *Wall Street Journal*, *Inc.*, and *Fast Company*.

Prior to forming Zenger Folkman, Joe was a founding partner of Novations Group, Inc., where he led the employee survey and 360-degree assessment practice. Joe holds a doctorate degree in social and organizational psychology, as well as a master's degree in organizational behavior from Brigham Young University.

He is a best-selling author/coauthor of 11 books and a sought-after speaker, consultant, and executive coach with the ability to connect with audiences through compelling research and inspiring stories.

If you'd like to learn more about Zenger Folkman's assessments and development experiences on TRUST and other leadership behaviors, please visit zengerfolkman.com.